PROSPERITY'S PREDATOR

BY

JOHN COOLEY

~~~~~~~~~~~~~~

"If, from the more wretched parts of the old world, we look at those which are in an advanced stage of improvement, we still find the greedy hand of government thrusting itself into every corner and crevice of industry, and grasping the spoil of the multitude. Invention is continually exercised, to furnish new pretenses for revenues and taxation. It watches prosperity as its prey and permits none to escape without tribute." ~Thomas Paine

~~~~~~~~~~~~~~

CONTENTS

3

FOREWORD

Government is both simple and exceedingly complex. At base, government is simply a way for people to join together to accomplish tasks that would be beyond the capacity of individuals. There are, of course, a number of ways to do this, other than government. Community organizations, churches, corporations and fraternal groups, to name a few, all perform this function in an assortment of venues.

Government differs from other organizations in that it wields the power of inclusion – that is, the power to enforce all persons in its sphere of influence to belong, unlike churches, corporations or social groups in which belonging is voluntary. The power of inclusion arises from two sources, which are complementary: the ability to create laws and the ability to enforce them. This is the essence of government. The ability to enforce laws comes from simple force, a necessity to protect government (and those it governs) from outside interference by other governments, while the ability to create laws flows from the ability to enforce them.

If government was limited to the creation and enforcement of simple laws, the keeping of order and protection of the governed, there would be little opposition to it, and it would be generally viewed as a beneficial organization conducive to prosperity. Unfortunately, the possession of power in any organization run by humans will be abused, as there is a genetic predisposition of people to seek power, wealth and self-aggrandizement. From this predisposition comes a continual pressure in any government to grow and expand its reach into the affairs of its subjects and into their pocketbooks. As government grows, its complexity increases, obeying the laws that govern the growth of any organism. The U.S. Constitution was designed with these considerations in mind, and it has been unusually successful in keeping the growth and intrusiveness of government in check. In the past century, however, human nature has once more raised its ugly head and government has undergone a rapid expansion, much of it in defiance of the Constitution.

Government, in general, is under the operant impression that it should govern us. It shouldn't be. Governing us is our job; government should be simply the tool that we use to accomplish that task.

In this small book I have addressed a number (by no means exhaustive) of the typical problems with the U.S. government, while realizing that these problems are actually rather generic to all governments. Each of these addresses ends with a short summary, and most are followed with a general suggestion on a possible palliative approach, some of which will, doubtless, be considered odd or radical. I have also thrown in an occasional light-hearted fictional short story about some of the more dismal problems.

The Author

DEMOCRACY

There is a vague notion that the United States is a democracy. It is not-- it is a republic. There is a difference. If you do not understand this difference, stop reading, go Google it and think about it. It's important.

Visualize a room with 100 people in it. 45 of them are women. One man proposes that any woman must submit to the attentions of any man at any time. The proposition is voted upon and passed by a majority of 55. This is very democratic.

Democratic election and policy making is all well and good if it is surrounded with rules and safeguards, and can be a useful social tool, but the vote is not a blessing from on high. Unfortunately politicians of all stripes and persuasions believe that a 53% popular vote is a mandate that allows them to ride roughshod over the wishes and desires of the other 47%.

Let's have a heads up here – having 47% of the populace pissed off at you cannot be good for anyone or anything, including the career of a politician.

Pure democracy is mob rule. Beware of the pitchforks.

Would it be unreasonable to require our schools to educate our children on the governmental structure of our country? Knowing the difference between a democracy and a republic is pretty basic, and knowing *why* we are a republic rather than a democracy is more important. It is even of greater importance that our politicians understand it, and it appears that a fair percentage of them do not.

LAFFER AND HANSEN

In 1980 an economist, Mr. Laffer, famously expounded the idea that there was a relationship between the percentage of taxation and the return to the government in actual revenues. At base, the idea, generally referred to as the "Laffer Curve", states the obvious, that at a zero taxation rate, the government receives no revenue, for no taxes are collected, and conversely, at 100% taxation the government collects no revenue because nobody will work to generate a tax base in the complete absence of reward.

Firstly, to give a bow to historical accuracy, Mr. Laffer did not originate the concept of the Laffer Curve. The Muslim polymath scholar Ibn Kaldun first expounded it in 1377. That being said, it must be admitted that there is somewhat more than theoretical support for the concept that between the obvious extremes there exists a curve of indeterminate, perhaps variable, shape. If an economy is on the downside of the curve, added taxes will decrease revenue, on the upside of the curve, additional taxes will increase revenue, a concept that appears to be borne out to some extent by increases in revenue after tax cuts, as in the Kennedy and Reagan presidencies. There does not, however, appear to be any sort of obvious 1:1 relationship between tax cuts, tax increases and government revenue.

The Laffer curve, it has been pointed out, is remarkably similar to the profit curve, where there is a point of maximum profitability between maximum sales at cost (zero profit) and a price so high that no sales occur (also zero profit).

There is, however, an interesting observation that is quite striking: the tax revenue of the United States is very consistent at about 19.5% of GDP (Gross Domestic Product), a correlation that has held true ever since such records have been kept. This relationship was first elucidated by an economist by the name of Hauser, and is often referred to as Hauser's Law, even though it is more of a datum than a true law. This does, however, explain the results seen from the increases and decreases of taxes, as these affect the GDP, creating the apparent uncertainties of the Laffer Curve. It would be more apropos to state that the Laffer Curve is an expression of the effect of taxes on the GDP, and that the much-disputed "ideal" point of most effective taxation on the Curve is, indeed, 19.5%.

The government should be constrained to live within its means.

The truly frightening aspect of Hauser's Law, however, is that *all spending by the Government above 19.5 % of the GDP will result in a deficit, which will become long-term debt, and that such debt cannot be paid off without spending dropping below the 19.5% mark. Spending should always be less.* The Fed, of course, has found another recourse – it simply prints money, thus monetizing the debt. This is not an advisable course, regardless of what any politician may think or desire. A commodity based monetary system would cure this problem, and fiscal control, possibly a Constitutional amendment limiting the income of the government, would bring a measure of sanity to governmental expenditures.

THE VISION THING

It should be noted that, by and large, politicians are imbued by "vision". That is, they have a vision of the great good things that they can do with their power and other peoples' money. The "visions" of politicians are almost never expressed in concrete terms, which is to say that their connection with reality is somewhat tenuous. They are, instead, set forth in general, glowing terms, which are peculiarly susceptible to being internalized by listeners. This type of phrasing and exposition is a learned art, and its mastery has direct effect upon the fortunes of political personages.

The congruity of any given politician's internal vision with the needs and desires of his or her constituents is probably a matter of happenstance and, as a general rule, is proven to be minimal. This leads politicians and legislators to pursue their own agendas in the fond belief that what they do is not only the will of the people, but also what is best for them. When external information in the form of unfavorable polls, public protests and grassroots opposition develops, it is the concept of the people's will that is sacrificed, and the politician will act on the basis of what he believes is good for the people, lamenting all the while over their obduracy and ignorance. In short, the vision triumphs over reality. The truly dangerous part of this is that the politician or legislator then becomes certain that he is not only wiser than the people, but that he should seek more power in order to better serve the people. This soon devolves to the point that the only remaining consideration is the power.

It is in this manner that good intentions are corrupted.

Power corrupts. The greater the power the greater the corruption.

The process of political corruption takes time, but it is inevitable. Persons of strong character recognize the danger of contagion and limit their exposure to the occasions and temptations. It is notable, as well, that the propinquity of already corrupted individuals speeds the corruptive process in others. These problems were greatly on the minds of the Founding Fathers of this nation and their concept of a citizen government with a governing body that met only briefly and when needed, was a bulwark against the problem. Keeping the terms of legislators short and their careers brief would alleviate the problem and minimize the chances for corruption.

DEEP POCKETS

The United States has about 6% of the world's population. It also is home to about 60% of the world's lawyers. The single largest occupation amongst legislators and politicians is attorney. Sober reflection on these three facts explains a persistent problem in our legislatures, to wit: the laws of the United States tend to be inimical to business interests and favorable to legal interests: this problem has shown every indication of increasing rapidly in the past couple of decades.

The root of the problem can be found in the perceptions of civil attorneys. When people suffer a loss, are hurt, insulted or physically injured, there is an innate human tendency for people to look for someone to blame rather than to take responsibility unto themselves. Placing a cup of hot coffee, in a Styrofoam cup, between your legs while driving can, in the hands of a good attorney, turn the resulting burns into an actionable case against the vending restaurant. The attorney is trained to search for a person or organization who meets two criteria in any case: they must be either blamable or share the blame and they must have "deep pockets", which is to say they must have sufficient wherewithal to indemnify the plaintiff and to pay the fees of the attorney. This mindset extends to grouping large numbers of people with a common minor complaint into "classes" and suing corporations on their behalf, winning millions for the attorney(s) involved and meaningless rewards, usually discount certificates, for the actual individual plaintiffs.

Quite aside from the rightness or wrongness of such procedures on the moral plane, the innate attitude implicit in the mind of attorneys is that companies, corporations, doctors and businesses are "to blame" in most adversarial legal proceedings (the companies, corporations, doctors and businesses generally being the ones with "deep pockets"). This attitude carries over into legislation composed by lawyers-become-legislators, much to the detriment of businesses and corporations.

Concentration of commonalities in legislators is dangerous.

We would reasonably become concerned if those making the laws were all farmers, suspecting that they might make too many laws too favorable to farmers. Nearly 45% of Congress is composed of lawyers. They make law favorable to lawyers, refuse to pass regulations or laws unfavorable to lawyers and stoutly oppose anything that smacks of tort reform. The situation has been thus for some time. We do, indeed, have reason to be concerned. Congress should be composed of persons from all walks of life, and having a concentration of those who, by training, are opposed to the free market endeavors that have brought prosperity to us for hundreds of years is a recipe for the decline of our country. A way to limit the over-representation of any vocation would be desirable.

CORRUPTION

Corruption in government is very expensive, the expense falling on the shoulders of those citizens who, by and large, are not corrupt. Corruption in government is at its worst in dictatorial regimes, as these offer the greatest opportunities for bribes, kickbacks and payoffs along with minimal risk of punishment. It is not too surprising, therefore, that corruption in any government tends to favor and abet a tendency toward dictatorship.

Recently there have been two notable earthquakes in densely populated areas. One was in Haiti and measured 7.0 on the Richter scale. The second was in Chili and measured 8.8 on the Richter scale. More than 230,000 people died in the Haiti quake, while less than 1200 died in the Chilean quake *and the resulting tsunami.* There was no tsunami in the Haiti quake. The Richter scale, that measures the power of an earth tremor, is a logarithmic scale: this means that the Chilean quake was nearly 18 times greater than the Haiti quake.

Why the huge difference in casualties between the two? The answer is both simple and disturbing: personal wealth. Haiti is a country that has been governed by dictators and near-dictators since before it became a country in 1804 and has been corruptly governed ever since with a series of dictators and overbearing "presidents" as well as a spell in the 1900s when the United States controlled the country, but did little to combat the corruption. Corrupt governments engender a climate of lax law enforcement, general disregard of such inconveniences as building codes and public safety rules, creating a climate in which free enterprise is severely hampered. This, in turn, means that there are few prosperous businesses and that corrupt officials extorting bribes and favors soon destroy those few that manage to develop. This makes for a generally poor populace, due to lack of jobs, and a poor populace cannot afford sound housing and safety devices. The lack of general wealth translates into inadequate and unsafe buildings, poor or non-existent medical and rescue services along with a general attitude of personal helplessness. When disaster strikes the shortcomings go on display.

While nations across the globe send aid teams to Haiti, with massive relief supplies and charity assistance that will probably extend itself for years after Chili has recovered, nobody talks about the root causes, and the corrupt, self-centered government responsible.

Chief amongst the benefits of a non-corrupt society are wealth and safety.

It is not a coincidence that wealthier nations suffer less from both natural and man-made disasters. Wealth furnishes the wherewithal to purchase safety in the form of good buildings, medical and disaster services. Public corruption, especially corruption under autocracies, creates poor societies and prevents them from improving by crippling free enterprise.

PROGRAMS

Ronald Regan once observed that immortality was best achieved by becoming a government program. There is considerable truth in this. Almost no program, once begun, is allowed to die. It may be transmuted into another program, but it will continue. The reason for this is obvious, even to the untrained observer, for programs are maintained by the persons for whom that program provides a living, and these persons are not only voters, but they are often union members and constitute a vocal minority, sometimes with their own K street lobbyists. It is in the interest of those employed in a program to try to further it, grow it and expand its reach.

Way back in August 4, 1977, a third of a century ago, under the Carter administration, the government established the Department of Energy. The intent behind it was reasonable, and all agreed that the DOE would solve one of the nation's more pressing problems. The DOE presently has grown to over 16,000 full-time employees plus more than 90,000 contract employees, with a budget of more than 24 billion dollars per year.

We all remember why that particular

department was started, don't we?

That's right; it was started for the purpose of decreasing our dependence on foreign oil.

How has that worked out for us?

Any government program should have a defined lifespan of no more than five years at the time it is established. If, after this lifespan, it is actuarially and performance-wise proven that any given program has not met its founding goals, it should not be renewed; if it has met these previously defined goals, then it will be given another few years of conditional life. No program should be conceived or continued without both a lifespan and a goal, as is illustrated by this bit of history.

~~~~~~~~~~~~

THE LOOKOUT

IN 1803, WITH NAPOLEON BONAPARTE DESTRUCTIVELY RAMPAGING ABOUT EUROPE, THE BRITISH GOVERNMENT, WORRIED (WITH SOME CAUSE) ABOUT THE POSSIBILITY OF AN ATTEMPT BY NAPOLEON TO INVADE ENGLAND, ESTABLISHED A SPECIAL OFFICE TO BE ON THE LOOKOUT FOR ANY SIGN OF A NAPOLEONIC INVASION FORCE. THERE IS NOTHING REMARKABLE IN THIS — INDEED IT WAS AN EMINENTLY REASONABLE THAT A PERSON SHOULD BE ASSIGNED TO SWEEP THE HORIZON, FROM ATOP THE WHITE CLIFFS OF DOVER, WITH A SPYGLASS, ALERT IN THE DAY FOR THE SAILS OF AN INVADING FLEET, AND AT NIGHT FOR UNTOWARD LIGHTS THAT MIGHT INDICATE THE SAME. IT WAS, AFTER ALL, A TIME WHEN THE EUROPEAN CONTINENT WAS IMMERSED IN WAR, AND ENGLAND WANTED NO PART OF IT APPEARING ON HER SHORES.

SO IMPORTANT WAS THE POSITION OF NAPOLEONIC LOOKOUT THAT IT WAS NOT ABOLISHED UNTIL 1947, 126 YEARS AFTER NAPOLEON DIED.

~~~~~~~~~~~~~

ADDING UP NUMBERS

Mr. Gomez owns a small store in Anaheim; it carries a modest line of home essentials, automobile service items such as oil and transmission fluid, an assortment of ready-to-eat foods, candy bars, beer, soft drinks, milk and a stand that displays fresh Cuban bread. It is similar to several tens of thousands of convenience stores across the nation.

This morning, as he does every day, he is taking an inventory of his needs. He is low on 30 weight motor oil, the bread sold out early yesterday, so he could request a half-dozen more loaves today, Goodie bars are low; he needs a fresh box and cola has been selling well. The days are getting warmer now, so he needs to increase his soft drink stock and cut back on the hot cocoa mix. In his half hour of inventory taking he makes 282 decisions, increasing, decreasing and modifying his stock to meet the needs of his customers. He does this every morning, as do the proprietors of 145 thousand small convenience stores all over the country. Approximately *thirty six million* decisions *every day.* In their various time routines, each in their own way, on their own schedules, every business in the country does the same thing. These billions of daily decisions of business keep the economy functioning smoothly, meeting various customer demands in a timely manner.

Politicians, as a whole, have never run, managed or started a business, have never met a payroll and have never run an inventory. They are, generally, a conceited lot, well convinced that they are wiser than other people by virtue of their having been elected. This combination is why they are convinced that they can manage an economy, and make it run more efficiently. They are sure that all of those convenience stores are identical, that customers buy from each of them in identical ways and in identical amounts, so simply putting a few persons in charge of telling the stores what they need and what they will get and what schedule they will get it on will increase efficiency, freeing up thousands of man-hours.

Of course, it doesn't work. It has been tried again and again, and has never worked. The numbers just do not permit it to work. Those thirty six million decisions made each day by convenience store owners are what *make* a convenience store a convenience store. Central government planning is attractive to politicians who lack even a rudimentary understanding of how the economic system works, but the power represented by putatively taking control has the same relation to them as honey does to bears. This is why Social Security, Medicare and the Post Office are going broke and why virtually all government programs produce little and cost much. Very large businesses often catch the same disease, but as they do not have the power of the tax, they frequently die of it.

Centralized planning is inefficient by nature, which is why the smallest possible government is the best government.

Most dictatorial governments tend to favor some flavor or other of Marxism and vice versa. The fact that central planning by an elite has never worked outside the small confines of a village or sailing ship seems to make no impression on such politicians, governments (or dictators). This is probably because being "in charge" is very important to them, and the more they can order the lives of others, the more important they feel. A few good psychologists could certainly devise a test (probably involving a polygraph) that could weed out such megalomaniac tendencies. A firm rule that no person could hold public office without passing such a test, in public view, would go a long way toward improving and limiting the grasp of our government. It should be noted that this would be a bit rough – a large majority of politicians are politicians because of these tendencies.

THE FEW AND THE MANY

All forms of government ever devised by man are hierarchical in structure, which is to say that they are shaped like a pyramid, with a single head of state at the top, whether that head is named king, president, prime minister or whatever title may be currently fashionable. There are however, two distinct *forms* of government. In the first one of these, power is spread over a relatively large number of individuals and is subject to the approval of the people at large, which is to say those at the base of the pyramid. There are a number of different flavors of this type of government; democracies, republics, constitutional monarchies, etc., but they still answer to this type of organization. In the second type, power is more concentrated into a fewer number of individuals, and these individuals are the ones who maintain power concentration in a restricted number at the top with little or no regard to those at the base of the pyramid. There are fewer flavors of this type of government, oligarchies, dictatorships, etc., but they all answer to this second type of organization.

Governments, of course, are relatively transient organizations. The United States is remarkable for its longevity of a couple of centuries. By contrast, the average lifespan of governments in Europe, taken as a whole during those two centuries, has been about thirty-five years. This means that governments change rather frequently. It is very difficult for a government to go from the second form of government to the first, simply because the few with the power at the top will not give it up easily. The First French Revolution of 1789 is an example of a change in this type. Changes typically come to such governments from the outside as war, either cold or hot, or from the inside as revolution. Changes from the first type to the second type of government come from the outside as war or from quieter political takeovers from inside. The rise of Hitler to power is an example of this type.

We need to be wary of power concentrations in politics.

A single dominant party can concentrate power in a few persons and convert the country into a dictatorship despite the Constitution. The fewer people in which the power is concentrated, the more dangerous and the more likely the conversion is to take place. In the United States the requisite number is probably less than a thousand. Congress, the President and appointed controllers, taken as a whole, are considerably fewer than that.

THE THINGS YOU GET AND THE THINGS YOU DON'T

Suppose you are interested in purchasing a new toaster. You shop around, online, by phone, in the paper. You locate exactly the toaster you want on line. You order the toaster, sending the vendor a check for $33.00, the price of the toaster and shipping charges, then await delivery with anticipation. Your check is cashed, but no toaster comes. You cannot relocate the on-line vendor: you have become the victim of a con artist, flim-flam man, or whatever term you choose. You have been ripped off. You have paid, filled your end of a contract, but the other end of the contract has not been honored. In simple terms, the vendor is a thief.

Suppose you own a store selling, say, hardware. One day a well-dressed man enters your store and tells you that you need to buy insurance against vandalism. The price is a mere 5% of your gross receipts. You turn down the offer. The next morning, when you come to open your store, you find it vandalized. Shortly after you repair the damage, the well dressed man returns. This time, you comprehend the wisdom of purchasing "insurance", and do so. This man, or the organization he represents, is also a thief, although a thief of a different sort.

There are many varieties of thief.

Governments do much the same as the above examples. They promise a benefit in return for your yielding money to them then often do not deliver, or they take a portion of your revenue under threat.

The conclusion is obvious: governments are, pretty universally, thieves. This is necessesary because governments, by their nature, are non-productive organizations and must prey on productive ones for their subsistence.

The problem is, that when governments offer services, those services *must* be accepted and paid for by all eligible persons; there is no choice. In theory, it should be possible for governments to offer their services to those who might be interested and allow others to decline, as the Post Office does, but that would place government in competition with private enterprise, a competition that government almost always loses (witness the effect of UPS, DHL and Fed Ex on the Post Office). Government therefore uses its power to force the purchase of benefits which some may not want, and pays for them with monies extracted by threat from all.

There are many varieties of thief.

The fact that every government is based on theft, and must finance itself through theft, should be regarded as intolerable. The obvious solution, of course, is to make the government into a service-based organization; this is to say that the government would provide those few services that *only* a powerful centralized organization can provide, and would charge specifically for each of those services, and only to those wishing them. The most obvious of these is national defense, which should be a concern of all citizens, followed closely by monetary and justice systems. Protection and regulation of the commons might also fall under government purview. While the financing of justice and monetary systems should present no problems – the money being paid by a discount on the issuance of currency and the justice system by the users, the support of the military would probably require a universal tax or conscription.

CRABS IN A BUCKET

Envy is a very common human emotion, and a very destructive one. It is no wonder that it is identified as one of the seven deadly sins. Normally civilized people keep this emotion under control. Oh, we may have a flash of envy over the skill (and luck) of an angler, the looks of a movie star, the wealth of a great baseball player or the possessor of a new car, but these are transient emotions, and we dismiss them readily. Unfortunately, envy, unlike most of the six other deadly sins, is susceptible to deliberate manipulation from outside, and is peculiarly resistant to criticism. There is a type of politician that takes advantage of these facts.

The politics of envy is well formed, and is almost always directed at "the rich". What is not immediately obvious is that any given individual's identification of who is "rich" generally refers to any person financially better off, it being universally presumed that the greater wealth was gained by luck or chicanery. The problem, of course, is that there is always someone richer than any given individual; hence envy can be excited in an entire populace without accurately defining those envied. There is, additionally, an easily aroused suspicion that the wealthy obtained their wealth by robbing the poor (as unlikely as that appears in print). The big attraction for politicians is that envy of wealth is easily encouraged and generates a popular desire to relieve the possessors of wealth of either all or a large portion of their riches by funneling the money into politician's pockets. While many of those who are envious expect that some of the wealth will devolve onto them, they are equally glad that the high have been brought low.

If you ever go crabbing, you will need only two implements: a dip net and a bucket. You do not need a top for the bucket. As you drop crabs into the bucket, and it begins to fill, an occasional crab will reach up for the rim of the bucket with intent to escape. You need not worry about a lost crab, however, as the other crabs will pull the escapee back down. This is the way the politics of envy works.

Isn't it amazing that poverty is blamed on those who have worked themselves out of it?

Envy is a very human emotion, and it is certainly completely outside of reason to think that we could eliminate it at its source, humanity being neither perfect nor perfectible. It is not entirely beyond reason, however, to suppose that we could make it off-limits in the field of politics. We have managed to eliminate (with a few rare and much-condemned instances) the use of racial epithets and sexual slurs once quite common in political campaigns. Appeals to class envy, wealth envy, etc. could well be eliminated in the same fashion. While this would undercut quite a number of political platforms and eliminate a number of favored phrases, the gain in political realism and the quieting of emotions would certainly improve the landscape of both political campaigns and legislative debate. It would be hard to suggest a tax on 'the rich' or regulation of 'greedy corporations' if appeals to envy and class were as much of an embarrassment as terms such as 'niggers' and 'queers' are today. We have done this sort of thing before, so there is no reason that we cannot do it again.

BANG BANG

Fort Hood, located near Killeen Texas, is one of the largest (in terms of population) U.S. military bases in the world. On November 5, 2009, one Nidal Hasan, a U.S. Army officer, shot and killed thirteen persons and wounded thirty. One *unarmed* reserve officer, Captain John Gaffaney attempted to stop Hasan, but was shot. Civilian police finally shot and arrested Hasan.

You should understand that the room in which Hasan did his shooting was filled with soldiers, military men and women, being readied to go overseas to the Afghan war. How did this happen? Certainly soldiers, trained for combat could have rapidly neutralized a lone shooter in plain sight and short range. Why was it *civilian police* that finally stopped him? It should be further noticed that Hasan was not combat trained, being a psychiatrist.

The answer is both interesting and disturbing. Soldiers, trained in combat and the use of weapons are not, by law, allowed to carry military weapons on their persons as a matter of routine, and any such bearing of weapons must be *permitted in writing*. It is further forbidden for military personnel to carry private (as opposed to military) weapons. This, of course, is pure idiocy, and is reflective of the unthinking, emotional idea that somehow guns kill people, quite independently of any operator. NOTICE TO ALL CONCERNED: people, not guns, kill people. Mr. Hasan had a nice safe barrel in which to shoot a whole bunch of people-fish.

A great deal of media/government publicity is being devoted to the question of why Mr. Hasan was not "detected" earlier, and why he was allowed to continue in his position. This is a smokescreen, which detracts from one of the basic questions: why are our military personnel unarmed? If the soldiers in that room had been routinely carrying weapons, it is unlikely that more than one person, other than Hasan, would have died. Can we lay these deaths on President Clinton's doorstep? Congress'?

If you wish to check on this seemingly insane policy, please refer to Army Reg. 190-14. Signed into law by President Clinton, effective Apr. 12, 1993.

Going armed is a Constitutional right denied even to those who protect the Constitution against "all enemies, both foreign and domestic".

The government and the Constitution have become mortal enemies. The Constitution is losing. The oath, taken by all military and government officials, states that they are obligated to protect the Constitution "against all enemies, both foreign and domestic". The oath should be taken much more seriously by all concerned. The present government could reasonably be considered a domestic enemy of the Constitution.

DEATH BY DUCK

The Constitution was laid out as the bedrock upon which the United States was to be built. It set forth a set of basic laws, explained the parliamentary procedures to be followed and, most importantly, erected a series of barriers and guards intended to prevent the government from encroaching upon the rights of the people. All in all, the founding Fathers did a remarkable job, but no construct of man is perfect.

When the Constitution was written, the southern states refused to accept it unless additional votes were given to them for the slave population. Eventually a compromise was reached, stating that "other than free persons" would be counted as 3/5 of a person when it came to voting. When the question of slavery combined with the economic pressures between northern and southern states came to a head in the late 1850's two factors underlay the secessionist movement: the question of slavery and the lesser question of state's rights. The South was wrong on slavery and correct on state's rights. Unfortunately, when it lost the war it lost both issues, and the ascendancy of federal power began, as Washington started to coalesce control, with theorists such as Lois Brandis advocating for centralized control by trained professional managers (bureaucrats). Bit by bit, the central government has taken more and more of the state's rights, until they have only a ghost of their original powers.

With the advent of Progressivism in the late 1890's and 1900's, the pace quickened, and the first real bites out of the Constitution began. The pace of the nibbling on the Constitution has accelerated as the defensive bulwarks of the Founders have been overcome and the public has become anesthetized to the ongoing damage. It is probable that some 90 percent of the powers, rules and laws of the current Federal government would have been considered in violation of the Constitution by its authors.

Being nibbled to death by a duck is minimally painful, but you still wind up dead.

The Supreme Court was established by the Founders to protect the Constitution and to prevent its corruption by the forces of the other two branches. The judges of the Court were given lifetime cinctures to, hopefully, prevent political corruption. Unfortunately, the judges are appointed and approved through the political processes that are the chief progenitors of corruption. We would probably be better off if they were selected by a random appointment from the general population, as they have been instrumental in finding supposed rights in the shadows cast by the Constitution, and in upholding blatant Constitutional violations in response to political pressure. To pretend that any body appointed through the political process can be neutral, adhering to strict law and logic is to believe in the Tooth Fairy.

TANSTAAFL

Things have value. "Things" may refer to material objects, ideas or labor. Even a pile of garbage has some kind of value. It is well to keep this principle in mind at all times; it insures you against the con man and the hard sell.

Politicians, like any slick salesman, may try to make you believe that you can get something for free if you will only vote for him (or her), accept the latest governmental proposal, or agree with the latest pronouncement. The politician, however, slides right past the fact that things have value, and since things have value, somewhere, somewhen, they must be paid for. In the case of government, not only must the things promised be paid for, but the cost of the government must be paid for as well. The salesman, con man and government always get paid off the top. This is the reason that government operated programs and services inevitably cost more than equivalent free market programs and services; the free market is forced by competition to minimize overhead, while government has every incentive to expand and increase overhead.

While government goods and services certainly must be paid for in money, government is also interested in one other commodity - - - power. Governments desire power because that is the commodity that allows it to push programs and agendas. Once approved by those seeking a free lunch, the program or agenda will be enforced through the use of power. Power, like anything else, has value. Power is indistinguishable from freedom; if you give it up, you are the poorer for the loss.

Robert Heinlein, a well-known writer, coined the word 'TANSTAAFL', which is an abbreviation of '**THERE AINT NO SUCH THING AS A FREE LUNCH**'. The term refers to the practice of some taverns and bars in offering a "free" lunch with the purchase of drinks. The truth, of course, is that the price of the lunch is rolled into the price of the drinks - - - the lunch is not really free, the cost is simply concealed.

Beware the politician bearing gifts; there is always a price, and the price is always hidden.

Many politicians (if not most) assure us that this program or that law will not cost anything, or might save as much or more than the price of enforcement. There is one true test for such pronouncements: include in each legislative enactment an estimate of the ultimate cost per year, in constant dollars, of the rule, law, program, etc. with the ironclad notation that the entire legislation and all of its attendant effects will be repealed the moment that the estimate is exceeded. This requirement would naturally eliminate a large number of proposals immediately (remember, the income tax, when first approved, was stated to *never, ever* exceed 3%). A rule (Constitutional Amendment?) enforcing the inclusion of such a limitation would go a very long way towards installing faith and trust in our government and in our legislators.

THE FED

There is no greater theft enabler for a government than a central bank. In the United States that central bank is the Federal Reserve Bank (generally called simply "the Fed"). The reason that the Fed is a theft-enabler is that it can print money without limit. If a citizen were to do this it would be called counterfeiting, but the Fed engages in this regularly, and all the extra printed money simply decreases the value of the money already in circulation by dilution. Since the government gets to spend the extra money, it is in effect a tax paid by everyone who uses money. As this is being written, the Fed, in the past year, has increased the money supply by 120%. This means that the dollar you had in your piggy bank New Years 2009 is now only worth about 45 cents today. You have been taxed 55 cents on every dollar you own.

Marx realized that a stable currency was the backbone of capitalism and the prosperity that arose from it, and he therefore made the establishment of a central bank with the power to issue fiat money (money not backed by a commodity such as precious metals) a plank of his program to establish Communism and destroy the capitalistic system.

Our Founding Fathers recognized the importance of a stable currency, and, in the Constitution, established gold and silver as the mediums of exchange. The government has ignored this part of the Constitution and has dishonored its contract to keep a sound monetary system.

Gold and silver cannot be counterfeited. Government hates that.

There is one solution to this problem; a commodity backed stable dollar. Paper currency is counterfeit, regardless of who is doing the printing. Consider the problems inflation brings:

~~~~~~~~~~~~

CURRENCY

THE MAN ACROSS THE TABLE FROM MARTY WAS HUGE. BICEPS BULGED AND THREATENED TO TEAR THE SLEEVES ON HIS SHIRT AND HIS SHOULDERS STRAINED AT THE RESTRICTIONS IMPOSED BY HIS JACKET. EVEN HIS NAME, BRUNO, BORE A HINT OF VIOLENCE. THE LARGE SUITCASE AT HIS SIDE BALLOONED WITH ITS CONTENTS, AND THERE WAS NO DOUBT ON THE PART OF EVEN CASUAL OBSERVERS OF THE NATURE OF THE BUSINESS THAT WAS BEING TRANSACTED. BRUNO HOWEVER WAS CALM, WITH NO APPARENT CONCERN ABOUT THE POSSIBILITY OF THEFT.

MARTY WAS NOT INTIMIDATED BY BRUNO, FOR THEY HAD BEEN FRIENDS FOR A LONG TIME, AND HE WAS WELL AWARE THAT BENEATH THE POWERFUL WRESTLER'S PHYSIQUE BEAT A GENTLE HEART. IT WAS CERTAIN, THOUGH, THAT BRUNO'S APPEARANCE WAS AN ASSET, FOR IT CERTAINLY WAS POSSIBLE THAT AN ERSTWHILE THIEF MIGHT BE DETERRED BY HIS APPEARANCE MORE THAN ATTRACTED BY HIS DISTENDED SUITCASE. MARTY GESTURED TOWARD THE SUITCASE. "TENS?" HE ENQUIRED. BRUNO SHOOK HIS HEAD. "FIVES. WHAT DO YOU HAVE FOR ME?"

MARTY REACHED INTO HIS POCKET AND SLID A GLEAMING GOLDEN COIN ACROSS THE TABLE. BRUNO PICKED UP THE COIN, EXAMINED IT THEN SET IT BACK ON THE TABLE. "IT'S REAL," MARTY SAID. "DROP IT ON THE TABLE, YOU CAN TELL FROM THE SOUND."

BRUNO SHOOK HIS HEAD. "NO NEED TO

ATTRACT ATTENTION. I CAN TELL IT'S THE REAL THING. BET YOUR OLD LADY'S ON YOUR CASE, ENH? NEED SOME OF THE FOLDING STUFF?"

MARTY SHRUGGED. "YOU KNOW HOW IT IS WITH DAMES. THEY ALWAYS NEED MORE THAN MEN. THAT'S JUST THE WAY THINGS ARE."

BRUNO CHUCKLED. "BOY, DO I EVER." HE FINGERED THE COIN. "YOU WANT IT ALL?" MARTY NODDED. "CAN'T LET IT ALL GO FOR THAT," BRUNO'S FINGERS CARESSED THE COIN. "WHAT ELSE YOU GOT?"

RELUCTANTLY MARTY REACHED INTO HIS POCKET AND DREW FORTH ANOTHER COIN THAT GLEAMED SILVER IN THE DIM LIGHT. "IT'S A 1998," HE SAID. "HASN'T BEEN CLIPPED."

BRUNO NODDED AND SWEPT THE COINS INTO HIS POCKET WITH A SINGLE SMOOTH MOVEMENT. "SAY 'HI' TO MILDRED FOR ME, TELL HER TO ENJOY AND DON'T USE IT ALL IN ONE PLACE." HE STOOD UP.

MARTY LAUGHED AND JOINED HIM, PICKING UP THE SUITCASE. "YEAH, I'LL DO THAT, BRUNO."

***

MARTY PUSHED OPEN HIS DOOR. "HONEY! MILDRED, WHERE ARE YOU?"

"IN THE KITCHEN." CAME THE REPLY. "DID YOU SEE BRUNO?"

"YEAH, HE SAYS TO SAY 'HI.' I GOT FIVES. IT'S ALL HE HAD."

MILDRED, TALL, LEGGY, A DISHWATER BLONDE, CAME OUT OF THE KITCHEN. "HEY, THERE'S GREAT NEWS ON THE TV. THEY DID AN ARTICLE ON AN OUTFIT IN KANSAS THAT'S FIGURED

OUT HOW TO MAKE PAPER OUT OF CORN STALKS. CORN STALKS DON'T COME UNDER THE CARBON TAX LIKE TREES, SO MAYBE THE PAPER CRISIS WILL GO AWAY. THEY'RE APPLYING FOR A GOVERNMENT GRANT FOR FURTHER DEVELOPMENT."

MARTY SHOOK HIS HEAD. "A GOVERNMENT GRANT — THAT IDEA WILL DIE ON THE VINE. THE MONEY WILL GO OUT, INFLATION'LL GO UP AGAIN AND NOTHING WILL GET DONE. DAMN GOVERNMENT'S THE ONLY OUTFIT THAT CAN AFFORD TO CUT DOWN TREES FOR PAPER WITH THE CARBON TAX AND THEY WANT IT THAT WAY."

"I KNOW, I KNOW," MILDRED CALMED, "IN FACT EVERYONE KNOWS, BUT WE JUST GO ON MAKING DO." SHE OPENED THE SUITCASE.

"REMEMBER BRUNO WANTS US TO RETURN THE SUITCASE. I'LL TAKE IT WITH ME NEXT TIME." MARTY BENT TO HELP HER PICK UP THE PILES OF FIVE- DOLLAR BILLS THAT CASCADED FROM THE OPEN SUITCASE.

"I'LL REMEMBER," MILDRED SAID. "BRUNO'S A GOOD FRIEND. WE OUGHT TO HAVE HIM OVER FOR DINNER AGAIN SOME TIME. I LIKE HIS WIFE, SHE'S SMART AND FUNNY." SHE BEGAN TO STACK THE BILLS NEATLY INTO PILES. "THIS PILE GOES TO THE DOWNSTAIRS BATHROOM, THIS ONE GOES TO THE UPSTAIRS. PUT A FEW BY THE COMPUTER, UNPRINTED SIDE UP. I USED THE LAST ONE YESTERDAY FOR MY SHOPPING LIST." SHE EYED THE VARIOUS STACKS AND SIGHED. "TV SAID THAT THE NEW ISSUE OF BILLS WOULD BE SMALLER IN SIZE TO SAVE PAPER. STILL BE PRINTED ON ONLY ONE SIDE, THOUGH, TO SAVE INK."

MARTY LOOKED UP FROM HIS TASK OF ORGANIZING THE BILLS. "THEY SAY WHAT

DENOMINATION THAT THEY'RE UP TO NOW?"

MILDRED WRINKLED HER BROW. "UMM. I THINK THEY'RE GOING TO BE TEN MEGABUCK NOTES. I'M NOT SURE THOUGH. PROBABLY WORTH ABOUT TWO COPPER CENTS OR THREE ZINC CENTS EACH. WHAT DID YOU HAVE TO PAY BRUNO FOR THESE?"

"A SACAGAWEA DOLLAR AND A '98 DIME. UNCLIPPED, AND THE SILVER WAS STILL ON IT." MARTY PICKED UP ONE STACK OF FIVE-DOLLAR BILLS AND HEADED FOR THE BATHROOM.

~~~~~~~~~~~~~~~

DANEGELD

Back in the bad old days, when Vikings rode the seas and terrorized English seaside villages, a custom grew up in oft-raided towns of simply buying off the raiders with a payment of gold. This saved the towns the unpleasantness of being burned, their men being killed and their women raped. It suited the Vikings as well, since they no longer had to exert themselves in killing and burning. Rape was still optional. Such payments were referred to as 'Dane geld' – gold paid to the Dane. We refer to the custom today as a 'protection racket'. It was a favorite income producer for the Mob in the early part of the last century, and, to all accounts, still exists today.

There are only two requirements for operating a protection racket – a productive source of wealth and an entity with superior firepower. The entity with the superior firepower takes wealth from the producer by threat of harm. It does not matter the source of the harm threatened – the threat may come from the operator of the racket or from other outside sources; the only requirement is that the threat be credible. Now, the art of gaining wealth by operating a protection racket is to not take so much that the health of the producer is threatened, and not to remove it too rapidly. The victim, once skinned, must always be given time to re-grow new skin, otherwise the racket fails due to the demise of the victim.

The protection racket is basic to all governments, because there is always a credible threat from other governments. The threat, of course, does not stop at the border, as the power of government, from aboriginal tribe to superpower, is universally used to enforce internal rule, laws and tax collections. These enforcements are often seen as desirable or necessesary, at least by a large portion of the population, and are therefore accepted. If, however, rules and laws become too cumbersome and complex, and the resulting taxes become too great, there is a danger that the taxed citizenry will have insufficient time or wherewithal to grow fresh skin. Down this road lies the destruction of nations through impoverishment or revolt. All caution should be exercised, in adding new laws and taxes, that this limit is not approached, for there is little that can be done to reverse the process. Each law, each rule, each tax grows government, and governments do not voluntarily shrink.

The English who paid the Dane geld had a saying that expressed this fact:

'Once you pay Dane geld, you never get rid of the Dane.'

Government by threat should be considered as barbaric, which it is. It is the basis of power for the most primitive of governmental systems – "I can beat you up, so submit".

So ingrained in the character of all governmental entities is this concept, however, that it is simply assumed that any governmental system has ultimate power over the citizen. The way to change this is to reverse it, to make the government subservient to the citizen. This is actually the intent and function of the vote, but the vote has been found to be manipulatable. Modern technology, though, has presented another opportunity, which should be investigated: the ability to quickly poll the citizenry via electronic means. Perhaps a running electronic poll, an enlarged version of the more narrowly based polls by Gallup, Zogby and similar agencies, could give a running readout of citizen reaction to various government activities. A sliding poll could well indicate political shoals ahead for unpopular legislation or spell looming sidelines for incumbents.

The biggest problem to arise from such an arrangement would be the tendency for it to approach a democracy and become mob rule.

CREAM RISES

There are two common factors in virtually all government jobs, both mundane and exceptional: first, the firing of a government employee, whether city, county, state or federal, is extremely difficult. Reams of paperwork, arcane rules, unions and redundant legal protections stand between the underperforming employee and the street. The paperwork, rules, etc. have, of course, been added by the government itself; an interesting instance of the problems resulting from uncontrolled positive feedback. Secondly, government jobs are mostly routine and boring. They are well defined, often by voluminous rules and regulations, and offer scant room for originality, innovation or excellence. The military, fire and law enforcement are probably the main, if not only exceptions, and even those are generally burdened by tradition.

The combination of these two factors causes an interaction, which explains a great deal about governments.

Presume, for a moment that a new government agency is created. There are no employees, so the positions in the agency are advertised, and employees hired. Now the law of averages says that the persons hired will be of various sorts; some will be incompetent, many will be average, some will be above average, some will be highly competent, some unambitious, some ambitious. Now human nature comes into play, for those who are highly competent and/or ambitious will soon find that a boring job, that does not give rein to their abilities and ambition, is unsatisfying and they will leave to seek greener fields. Those leaving will be replaced by, once again, those with an average spread of talents and ambitions, whereupon the process repeats. Those of low competence, little ambition and below average will remain behind. This is a filter, selective of the marginal and unambitious. The end result is a government filled with jobholders, the unimaginative and the minimally competent. These persons, in turn, create additional paperwork, rules and laws to further secure their positions. So prevalent and established is this phenomenon that those seeking education aimed at one or another type of government employment find that their schooling is filled with rote learning and prescriptive behavior. Teaching and civil management are prime examples. This goes a considerable distance to explain the ponderousness of government functions.

Competence and efficiency are fostered by risk, not safety.

The cure for this problem is obvious; not only make the work more meaningful, but make the system of retention and promotion more like that of private enterprise. One of the major problems with this approach is that a large number of government workers are unionized, and the unions have considerable political clout. Ronald Reagan demonstrated, in his handling of the air traffic controllers' union, that the problem of a union need not override good management of public resources and money. The example is both instructive and a precedent.

THERE OUGHTA BE A LAW

How often have you heard people say; "there oughta be a law"? Probably you have said it yourself upon observing some particular problem or abuse. It is an almost universal human emotion, but examine it for a moment. In its essence, we are wishing that some other powerful party (the government 999 times out of 1000) would take action against one or more *other* persons to satisfy *our* desire to control the behavior of *others*. This is the base upon which socialism is built, and it is what makes it so attractive to so many. One never says it in hopes that someone will control *their* behavior. It eventually (and rather quickly) extends to taking *other* person's wealth and making it *ours*. That is a very short step from taking *another's* freedom and restricting it for *our* benefit. Socialism is simply selfishness projected by power. What we never seem to realize is that it is a two way street – we take from *others*, but *others* take from *us* by the same power. This is a downward spiral that ends with nobody having anything, except, of course, those who manage the power.

There *shouldn't* be a law. The fewer laws that we need, the freer we are.

The desire to make laws to cure every petty

problem or societal ill is endemic amongst legislators. It is what they do. This should be changed, so that legislators gain public acclaim by *decreasing* laws. Perhaps it would be a good idea to have a limit of, say, 1000 laws. To introduce a new law, legislators would need to eliminate another of lesser import. To make this work, it would be necessesary to limit each law to a single subject.

EAVENING OUT WEALTH

There is a persistent notion amongst people that the distribution of wealth should be more even, that for some to have great wealth while others are relatively poor is somehow wrong. This is the heart of the socialist philosophy; it levels things out by producing an even poverty (except for the few who are 'more equal' and run the system).

All wealth is the product of human activity. One man may pluck a gold nugget from the ground and become immediately wealthy, while another may labor for years at plowing, planting and harvesting crops to become no more than modestly well off. In this respect, there is indeed inequity. One man was lucky, the other industrious, and the lucky came out on top. Luck, however, is --- well --- *chancy*. Sitting down and waiting, like Candide, for a change in your fortunes is generally unproductive. If you were born in a country that is floating in oil, you are lucky; if you were born in Ethiopia, you are not. Chance aside, however, industriousness, intelligence and effort are the main producers of wealth. Politicians and their governments often cater to the belief that wealth should be more even, promising their people that the government will remove the wealth possessed by the rich and redistribute it to the poor, through taxation, universal health care, subsidized housing, welfare or whatever the latest popular target may be. Societies that opt for this type of system are called Socialist.

Apparently nobody thinks this through. If you are poor, and someone hands you money, it means that you will not need to work as hard. Therefore you will produce less through your labor. If you are wealthy, and your wealth is taken from you, you will work less, since you do not profit as much from your labor. Therefore you will produce less through your labor.

This is what is referred to as positive feedback, a race to the non-productive bottom. It quickly spirals to the point that everyone is equally poor and becoming poorer. The reality of this has been demonstrated again and again in real life, but the move works momentarily, until the wealth is dissipated, and momentarily is enough to get politicians and dictators into positions of power. Then, of course, it is too late to change back. This type of change is a ratchet - - - it only goes in one direction, for those receiving the largess will not let go of their dole and return to productive effort, nor will the politicians relinquish the power so gained, short of revolution.

It should be noted that no society has ever started out with a socialist economy and then risen to prosperity under it.

Socialism works until you run out of other people's money. (Margaret Thatcher)

The basic proposition here, that neither socialism nor communism have promoted prosperity, has been proven in history, experiment and logical modeling time and again, but it still finds almost slavish adherents in all societies and countries. Perhaps a workable solution would be to create a test group to try out the particular scheme being put forth by a given politician, drawing the population of the test group entirely from those who voted for the politician. If the scheme can be shown to be successful, then all is well to extend the concept to a larger field; if not, then only those enamored of the idea will bear the loss. This would also encourage the politician or legislator to consider the workings of his plan most carefully, lest he lose support when things go awry.

KELO

In 2005, the Supreme Court of the United States made a decision that opened the way for any government, national, state, county or city, to seize the real property of any citizen if it could be shown that there was a use for that property which would produce a greater tax revenue. This was the case of Kelo vs. New London Ct. (545 US 469) 268 Conn. 1,843.2d500.

The U.S. Constitution allows the government to "take" property, through the doctrine of eminent domain, for "public purposes". Kelo allowed the taking to extend to the eminent domain taking of property to be turned over to private interests, which would pay greater taxes. The background of this hearkens back to the Government exercising eminent domain to provide the railroads with rights of way across the country. Because of the huge benefits of the railroads, this passed with minimal comment. In both of these cases and others, however, the principle of private property was savaged. The basic problem here is that when government is given an inch in any arena, it shoehorns this into a mile. The Constitution gave the government a reasonable power, which, if used wisely, would be beneficial and would not seriously discommode anyone. This power has, predictably, been abused.

Private property of any sort should be beyond the reach of the government.

The ownership of property is a basic right of human beings, and is intrinsic to freedom. The Constitution made a reasonable limit on that right in the "takings" clause. The Founders did not reckon with the perfidy of government and its minions, however, and the manner in which the clause could be distorted far beyond its original intent. If government feels the need for a particular piece of real property, or property of any other type, let it bid for it on the open market. Through abuse, the government has forfeited its right to the "takings" clause. It should be negated through a Constitutional Amendment.

THE INTERNET

The advent of the Internet was a sudden phenomenon, and its offspring, cell phone communication, Twitter, Facebook and other fast social sites caught the ruling political class flatfooted. Governments, after all, move slowly, and a twenty-year rise to the immense level of popularity of electronic communication and information technology gave no time for the usual political reaction. If government had had a chance, it would have wrapped the Internet in rules, regulation and taxes the way it did the telephone and telegraph. There are half-hearted efforts in this direction even today, but the truth is that the size and extent of the Net has slipped from the bag, and no effort short of open warfare will return it. Fortunately, the government is ill equipped for any such venture; government websites are crude, unfriendly and easily overwhelmed. The recent federal 'cash for clunkers' program had such a lame site that it crashed with a few tens of thousand visitors. Even modest commercial websites easily handle such traffic loads on a regular basis; nor was the inefficiency ameliorated by the voluminous paperwork required.

The government's problem with the Internet, of course, is that it is rife with dynamic, inventive people communicating, talking, cooperating, being entertained, selling, buying, making and learning; millions of people on millions of computers. Government, on the other hand, is rife with placeholders and timeservers who understand or care little of this.

The Internet is an example of what happens when people are not under government control. The edges are rough, scam artists abound, things from gross to sublime, legal and illegal, beautiful to repulsive may be found there, but the Net is alive, brawling, growing, free and yeasty, reveling in an open and apparently unlimited future.

The Net is today what America was 200 years ago.

The government and politicians hate it. They will try to control it, tame it, restrict it, tax it and discipline it, make it predictable and safe. It remains to be seen whether or not they will succeed.

Safety is cheap -- all it costs is your freedom.

The government would do well to keep hands off of the Internet, if for no other reason than that it can provide a reference point to tell us what complete freedom actually means. This function as a reference point is probably the basic reason why the government abhors it. The most substantial means that the government has to regulate the Internet is that of taxation, but this edges into the territory of the constitutional provision against interstate tariffs and the first amendment and legislators, to date, have been unwilling to go there; additionally, there is the fact that the Internet crosses all international boundaries. This unwillingness probably will not persist in view of the lax attitude in Congress regarding the constitutional limits on power.

Other means of regulation may be sought by enlisting those who may stand to gain, at least temporarily, by suppression of the more offbeat aspects of the net. E-bay would be glad to see Craigslist shut down, and Microsoft would love to eliminate Linux. All users of the net should resist such attempts. Blogs, web pages and random users – all should bombard the in-boxes of any legislators, politicians and businesses that may be considering the least restriction of the net.

One person, acting alone will only irritate those who would take over the Internet, but millions, each taking only small and limited action will, in their cumulative strength, move mountains.

Freedom is at stake.

THE HACKER

Brenda Chang pushed back from her keyboard and swiveled around, the oversized leather chair making a slight squeak as she sat up straighter. "Those socialist pigs are going to do what!? I don't believe it! They can't do that. How in the hell could they tax the internet?"

Jerry spread his hands out in a subdued shrug. "They want to put a mil per kilobyte on all traffic. Monitor the servers, bill them and let them collect from the users."

"That's like charging tax on the phone system according to how many words are spoken. That's bullshit." Brenda drew her lanky frame up into the chair and rocked back. "That would make my week's work cost - - - holy shit! Almost five hundred! No way."

"And you're going to do what?" Jerry snickered. "I've told you and told you that the government's going socialist, and you just go 'ya, ya, I know what real socialism is 'cause I lived in China.' Well its here, baby, and this time the bite's going to come out of your ass."

"And everyone else's ass. This is going to hit everyone, and I mean everyone, not just programmers like me. On line businesses, e-mailers, gamers - - - OMG! This is going to put Putin out of business. You know how much traffic a game designer puts out? One little background feature might be

NINETY MEGS." SHE ROCKED BACK AND FORTH, THE CHAIR GIVING OUT A PROTESTING SQUEAK WITH EACH OSCILLATION. THIS, JERRY KNEW, WAS HER THINKING MODE. BRENDA WAS FAR BEYOND HIS REACH, IMMERSED DEEP IN HER THOUGHTS, PROGRAMMING LINES RUNNING THROUGH HER HEAD, TWISTING AND TURNING, MAKING NEW CHANNELS IN HER MIND. HE QUIETLY TIPTOED FROM THE ROOM.

***

THE THIRD ASSISTANT SECRETARY TO THE ADMINISTRATOR OF DOCUMENTS WAS PANICKED. "IT'S THE SAME EVERYWHERE. EVERY GOVERNMENT COMPUTER THAT'S ON LINE IS FILLED UP. THE DRIVE ON MY COMPUTER IS NEARLY A TERABYTE, AND IT'S FULL OF THIS GARBAGE." HE CLICKED HIS MOUSE AND THE COMPUTER SLUGGISHLY RESPONDED, DISPLAYING A COPY OF SNOW CRASH. "DIFFERENT STUFF ON EVERY COMPUTER, BUT IT'S ALL LIBERTARIAN NOVELS, POLITICAL TRACTS, THE FEDERALIST PAPERS, ALL SORTS OF JUNK. I HAD TECH SUPPORT UP HERE, THEY CLEARED IT ALL OUT, TOOK THEM ABOUT AN HOUR, AND AS SOON AS THEY WERE GONE, IT FILLED BACK UP AGAIN. WORST, THIS ALWAYS POPS UP ON THE HOME PAGE." HE STRUCK A KEY AND THE ILLUSTRATION OF A COILED SNAKE APPEARED WITH THE WORDS 'THE INTERNET' PRINTED ON IT. BELOW WAS THE TITLE 'DON'T TRED ON ME'. "THE WHOLE DAMNED GOVERNMENT'S ALMOST SHUT DOWN. NO E-MAILS, NO TAX RETURNS, NOTHING'S GETTING THROUGH."

***

JERRY WAS CURLED ON THE SOFA WITH BRENDA. "O.K. I UNDERSTAND ABOUT THE VIRUS

YOU GUYS DREAMED UP. IT JUST GOES OUT ON THE INTERNET AND HUNTS DOWN CONSERVATIVE TYPE ARTICLES, NOVELS, WHATNOT AND UPLOADS UNTIL THE HARD DRIVE IS FULL. BUT HOW DOES IT GET INTO THE COMPUTER, AND WHY DOES IT AFFECT ONLY GOVERNMENT COMPUTERS?"

BRENDA CHUCKLED AND SNUGGLED CLOSER. "THAT WAS PUTIN'S IDEA. THE VIRUS SPREADS TO ANY COMPUTER IT CAN, RIDING ON EVERY E- MAIL AND IS CONTINUALLY MUTATING SO THAT EVEN IF IT'S DELETED IT COMES BACK IN A NEW INCARNATION." SHE THOUGHT FOR A MOMENT. "PROBABLY FIFTY TO SIXTY PERCENT OF THE COMPUTERS IN THE WORLD ARE INFECTED, AND EVENTUALLY ALL OF THEM WILL BE. IT ATTACHES TO ANY AND ALL E-MAILS. IT ONLY GOES ACTIVE WHEN IT SEES THE APPROPRIATE E-MAIL RECEIVING ADDRESS. THEN IT STARTS UPLOADING, AND THE FIRST THING IT UPLOADS IS YOUR HANDSOME SNAKE." SHE GIGGLED. "OH, IT'S A BEAUTIFUL HACK, JUST BEAUTIFUL."

"WHAT IS AN APPROPRIATE E-MAIL ADDRESS?" HE ASKED, A BIT PUZZLED.

"WELL, YOU KNOW, THAT LAST BIT ON AN ADDRESS: .GOV"

~~~~~~~~~~~~~~

THE TWINS: MONEY AND POWER

People have an inherent, probably genetic, love of both money and power. Of course the two are entwined, for those with money but no power can use money to buy power, by means of bribes, while those with power but too little money can dispense favors in return for money.

Bribery is an endemic disease tied to power. Lower functionaries of government can be bribed with minor favors and even compliments, but as one rises upward through the ranks, the price increases accordingly. Thus it is that the first act of elected officials is generally to award their supporters with positions, power and gratuities. This would not be so bad, except for the fact that the price is paid by the taxpayers in general, almost never from the pockets of the elected official. Indeed, the official him (or her) self expects to reap rewards from the elective position. The rewards may be simple money, but more often is a series of stock tips, extraordinarily good purchases, gifts and sexual favors. And of course, power.

Amongst the elected classes it is considered that the sophistication of a civilization can be measured, at least in part, by the distance between the outstretched palm and the coin deposited therein. In cruder societies, the payment is overt and immediate, in more elite circles the check arrives in the mail. It is the height of naiveté, however, to believe that the transaction does not occur, despite copious laws against any such degradation of the public trust. All this gives the members of any ruling class blackmail power over each other, and if one offends a sufficient number of the others, that person may be assured that some or all of his transactions will be revealed as a matter of punishment, from the revelation of mistresses to the discovery of cold cash reserves stashed in unlikely places.

There is a general understanding and tolerance of all this amongst the general public, but that understanding gives a certain class of politician a great advantage if he promises to see to it that those who vote for him and his agenda will share in the wealth. This is one reason that socialism and communism find a certain appeal amongst those who would sell their birthrights for a bit of pottage.

It is doubtful that there has ever been a poor dictator.

It is probably impossible to separate money from politics, and power is inherent in the political process. The question, then, is how to defuse these two. Endless laws, ethics statements, etc. etc. have been proposed and enacted with virtually no effect, in attempts to control money in politics, so that may be a dead end, although a law stripping any legislator of all wealth and requiring that person to live all of their life on a public dole equal to the average income of all citizens might work.

Some means to hold political power in disrepute would also be advantageous. Reagan observed that politics was the second oldest profession, and held a great resemblance to the oldest profession. Perhaps fostering a similar public perception of all politics would be constructive.

AUTHORITY

Government employs large numbers of people. Indeed, one of the inherent goals of government is to increase the number of persons employed, as power in government positions is, in substantial part, measured by the number of persons under you, that is to say by the number of persons over whom you have authority. During recessions, when people are losing jobs and businesses are cutting positions to retrench, government generally grows, adding jobs.

Now, to deal with government is to deal with ranks of persons, each jealous of their own small (or large) portion of authority. To challenge or dispute the authority of a governmental worker is to challenge the very reason for their existence. This frightens them on a fundamental level; remember that these are, by and large, persons of restricted abilities, used to secure and rote jobs. This same problem exists in private companies, but to a considerably lesser extent, because in private enterprises it is recognized as unproductive and inimical to the acquisition and retention of customers. When you deal with government, however, you are a captive customer –you *must* deal with that office – there is no competition to go to.

This mindset is prevalent and endemic at all levels of government and accounts to a fair extent for the glacial speed of government actions, as well as the frustration of those who must perforce deal with government offices.

Whoever has authority over you, no matter how small, will use it.

The petty abuse of authority is a constant irritant when dealing with governmental entities, and it is made more irritating by the basic fact that it is safer for a government functionary to say "no" than to take the responsibility of saying "yes". A simple solution would be to make the continuation of a government employee's job dependent on the performance of that job *as viewed by the persons with whom the employee deals,* rather than the status of his union or the difficulty of firing the employee. An ongoing public poll of the functionary's performance, evaluated by the "customer", would certainly change the mindset if that evaluation determined raises and even retention. Good luck keeping that from being corrupted, however!

OXEN

On the whole, people like to be left alone to pursue their lives in peace. The shopkeeper wants to open his store in the morning, sell to and chat with his customers, close and go home to his or her family. The farmer wishes to till his field, plant and harvest. The scientist and scholar want to pursue their studies in serene confidence that they are benefiting the world at large. Unfortunately there are those in the human population who feel that it is their right to interfere with the lives of other persons, to direct and control them. If this is a single person, say a robber, rapist or burglar, a well-placed bullet will generally restore the peace and eliminate the problem. When, however, a number of such like-minded individuals get together they can convince a significant number of others to join their way of thinking and to engage in acts that they would otherwise abhor. This is why it was easy to recruit death camp guards in WW II Germany. Fear of the consequences is sufficient to silence the remainder of honest citizens. These social divisions, once established, maintain and enlarge themselves, attaining a life of their own. The groups so formed can be isolated and made cohesive by their predation on outsiders. The leaders encourage this.

It is notable that those who successfully recruit others to join in their antisocial activities generally do so via the avenue of politics for, through politics, power may be obtained with minimal personal risk. Granted, some few rise to their ambitions through pure power, but these are rare exceptions, and were much more prevalent in the distant past when sword and mace were strong persuaders.

History is replete with instances of the violent and antisocial abuse of power, but it is noticeable that, while condemning them, few political cabals do more than use such instances as arguing points for their own ambitions to power. After all, those examples held up by history were *them* not *us*. *We* are the important ones now, not *them*, and most certainly the instances of abuse today are far removed from those odious examples from history.

Israel, America, Europe and yes, even Germany, looked at the Holocaust, the fruit of a National Socialist government, and agreed "never again". Then Russia, Rwanda, Cambodia and Darfur came and passed with a shrug. Those cases were, of course, *them*, not *us*.

It, indeed, matters whose ox is being gored.

The lessons of history are hard to learn, and we should never consider that they do not apply to us. Concentrations of people with a common agenda are, regardless of agenda, dangerous, for the commonality leads to a narrowed and restrictive outlook that tends to favor the "hammer" approach (if all you have is a hammer, everything starts to look like a nail.) This is one of the basic problems with political parties. We might well be better off if we elected individuals as individuals, rather than as members of a party, forcing legislators to seek a consensus view of reality rather than a "party" view.

TOO BIG TO FAIL

Somewhere, somewhen, somebody came up with the idea that some institutions were "too big to fail". The concept here was that some businesses were so large and involved so many persons and controlled so much wealth that their failure would be so catastrophic that it would be to everyone's interest to prop them up and prevent them from failing. This, of course, flies in the face of the basic principles upon which all businesses should operate. Business failure is the way that the marketplace tells businesses that they have not served their customers properly.

When businesses fail, they do not simply evaporate. The pieces are not lost. The capital equipment is purchased by other businesses, the customers find others to serve them, and workers find jobs in new businesses that replace the failed business. This is a natural, one might say organic, process, just as trees in a forest grow, age, fail and die, making room for new trees when they fall. It is a natural winnowing process that assures that only the best services and products survive. Interference with this process, no matter how urgent it may appear, results in inferior services and products and wastes the general wealth. Rescuing a failing business may, indeed, prevent the momentary loss of jobs and assorted injuries to other businesses dependent on the failing enterprise, but the long-term cost is invariably many times greater, albeit hidden from general view.

It should be no surprise that the government, at the behest of politicians, is the usual agency for propping up those "too big to fail". The message sent is a fatal one: 'we will protect you – you may be lazy, dishonest, inefficient, produce bad products and give poor service, but –we will protect you.'

Size does not assure survival. Just ask Goliath.

Businesses and institutions are not immortal constructs. In the general interest they must be allowed to compete, live and die. Size is not necessesarily a survival trait. It didn't work for the dinosaurs and it shouldn't work for human creations.

RIGHT AND WRONG

It can be fairly argued that the ability to invent, produce and market, much as the ability to grow, reap and sell food, is a prime driver of prosperity. Those who make the goods that permeate our society are, in large part, responsible for what is usually referred to as our 'advanced standard of living'. Our marketplaces are replete with items to satisfy every want and appetite and the supply is driven by persons and companies who seek to sell to us, the consumer. Competition and the free market drive to profit and succeed has given us wide screen TVs, warmed and cooled our homes, infused our universities, produced medicines to vanquish the plagues of the ancients, given us arts and theater to entertain the world, and allowed us to access the deepest and widest wells of knowledge. In the midst of this vast cornucopia of wealth is snuggled the government tax collector, and for each item that tumbles into the waiting arms of customers a bit is scraped off in taxes. They may be excise taxes, tariffs or sales taxes, but they all come to the same thing: a tax upon prosperity.

To take something away from a person is usually considered a punishment. We take freedom away from the criminal by confining him or her, we fine the person who exceeds the speed limit, costing them money and time. This is a well-established principle that can even extend to taking away life in some instances.

A fine is a tax for doing something wrong.

A tax is a fine for doing something right.

Taxes, as we have observed, should be related to function, not randomly placed on this or that product of man's ingenuity or labor.

Admittedly, it is easier to tax all electronics sold than, for example, to tax TVs, radios and cell phones to provide for the regulation of the electromagnetic spectrum while leaving toasters and electronic games untaxed, but that is the reasonable, just and honest way of operating.

Government would be smaller, more useful and much better regarded if it operated in this way.

~~~~~~~~~~

THE AUDIT

THE DARK SUIT AND THE BLUE TIE WERE ALMOST A GIVEAWAY IN THEMSELVES, WITHOUT THE LITTLE IRS CARD. MARCUS' HEART DID A QUICK SKIP-BEAT AND BILE ROSE IN HIS THROAT. HE KNEW THAT HIS ACCOUNTANT WAS CAREFUL AND KEPT HIS BOOKS IN METICULOUS ORDER, BUT HE ALSO KNEW THAT NOBODY COULD UNDERSTAND ALL THE IMMENSITY OF THE IRS TAX LAW, MUCH LESS THE CONVOLUTED LOGIC OF ITS APPLICATIONS. NONETHELESS HE INVITED THE AUDITOR IN AND OFFERED HIM A SEAT. "WHAT CAN I DO FOR YOU MR. - - -" HE LOOKED AT THE LITTLE CARD, "MR. SMITH?" HE WAS SURE THAT THE NAME WAS FALSE, BUT HE SMILED ANYWAY.

MR. SMITH PLACED HIS COMPUTER ON THE DESK AND OPENED IT. "I WILL NEED TO SEE A DISC OF YOUR BOOKS. STANDARD FEDERAL GOVERNMENT FORMAT."

"SURE, JUST A MOMENT." MARCUS SORTED THROUGH A NUMBER OF DISCS

ON HIS DESKTOP. "HERE'S THE LATEST TRANSCRIPT."

MR. SMITH LOOKED DISPLEASED. "A TRANSCRIPT? YOU DON'T KEEP YOUR BOOKS ON DISC IN STANDARD FEDERAL GOVERNMENT FORMAT?"

MARCUS SHOOK HIS HEAD. "NONE OF THE NEW COMPUTERS COME WITH THE OLD CD DRIVES ANYMORE, THEY ALL USE FLASH STORAGE STICKS. OUR ACCOUNTANT USES BOSTON ACCOUNTING

SOFTWARE. WE KEEP AN OLD CD BURNER FOR YOUR RECORDS. BOSTON SOFTWARE HAS A CONVERSION PROGRAM TO REDUCE OUR RECORDS TO SFGF AND BURN THEM TO DISC. IT'S GETTING DIFFICULT TO GET THOSE OLD CD DISCS NOWADAYS."

MR. SMITH NODDED. "THE GOVERNMENT LIKES THE RELIABILITY OF THE OLDER SYSTEMS." HE SLIPPED THE DISC INTO HIS COMPUTER. THERE WAS, MARCUS NOTED, NOTHING OLD ABOUT THE COMPUTER, A GLEAMING NEW TOBASHI WITH A VIRTUAL KEYBOARD. SMITH MOVED HIS HANDS BRIEFLY OVER THE KEYBOARD AND A DISPLAY LIT UP ON THE SCREEN. HE LEANED FORWARD, STUDYING IT INTENTLY. "WELL, IT APPEARS THAT YOU MADE A PROFIT LAST YEAR, WHICH YOU REMITTED, QUITE PROPERLY, TO THE GOVERNMENT. YOU DID, HOWEVER, BUY A STERILIZER. WHAT EXCUSE DO YOU HAVE FOR SUCH AN EXPENDITURE? YOU RUN A KNIFE SHARPENING BUSINESS."

MARCUS BEGAN TO TREMBLE. "IT --- IT'S FOR THE MEDICAL STUFF. THEY DON'T THROW AWAY SCALPEL BLADES, NEEDLES AND CUTTING INSTRUMENTS, THE WAY THEY DID BEFORE THE GOVERNMENT TOOK OVER THE MEDICAL INDUSTRY. NOW THEY SEND THEM OUT TO BE RE-SHARPENED. WE NEED TO STERILIZE THEM BEFORE AND AFTER SHARPENING, BEFORE TO PROTECT OUR WORKERS FROM DISEASES THAT MIGHT BE ON THE BLADES, AND AFTER SO THAT THEY WILL BE STERILE FOR USE. IT'S A WHOLE NEW AREA OF BUSINESS FOR US. IT'S WHY WE MADE A SMALL PROFIT LAST YEAR."

MR. SMITH SHOOK HIS HEAD. "I DON'T SEE THAT. YOU SHARPEN THINGS. THE GOVERNMENT WON'T ALLOW YOU TO JUST HARE OFF INTO OTHER

BUSINESSES WITHOUT PERMISSION. YOU WILL NEED TO FILL OUT FORMS BSTF- 786 AND BSTF-9766, AND I CANNOT ALLOW YOU TO DEDUCT THE EXPENSES OF THE STERILIZER OR THE TIME, OVERHEAD AND LABOR ASSOCIATED WITH IT. FILL OUT THE FORMS, SUBMIT THEM AND THEN, IF THEY ARE APPROVED, YOU CAN BEGIN TO DEDUCT EXPENSES NEXT YEAR."

MARCUS SANK INTO HIS CHAIR. "THAT WILL PUT ME OUT OF BUSINESS. THERE'S NO WAY THAT I CAN PAY DOUBLE FOR THE MACHINE, MY LABOR AND EXPENSES. I FILLED OUT FORMS LIKE THAT ONCE BEFORE; IT TOOK THREE HUNDRED HOURS AND IT TOOK TWO YEARS FOR APPROVAL."

"NOW, SIR, DON'T TAKE THAT ATTITUDE. THE GOVERNMENT WON'T LET YOU GO OUT OF BUSINESS. WE WILL MANDATE THAT YOU AND ALL OF YOUR EMPLOYEES CUT BACK YOUR SALARIES, SAVING A CONSIDERABLE AMOUNT, AND YOU WILL BE ELIGIBLE FOR A SMALL BUSINESS LOAN FROM THE SBA. JUST FILL OUT FORMS SBA 99-66 AND SBA 4441-B. WE CAN'T LET YOU GO OUT OF BUSINESS; THERE ARE TOO MANY UNEMPLOYED PEOPLE OUT THERE WHO NEED YOUR MONEY. IT'S NOT RIGHT THAT YOU AND YOUR EMPLOYEES CAN MAKE A LIVING BY WORKING WHILE OTHERS DON'T HAVE THAT OPPORTUNITY." MR. SMITH STOOD UP, CLOSED HIS COMPUTER AND HEADED FOR THE DOOR. "DON'T FORGET TO FILL OUT THE PROPER FORMS", HE ADMONISHED.

BOO!

People love to be frightened as long as they know that there is no real danger. This accounts for the popularity of monster movies, gothic novels, visions of Armageddon and earth-meteor collision tales. This love does not extend to real fears. People do *not* love fear. Politicians are well aware of this.

Raising a boogieman is an ancient political tactic, and has always been effective. It is also easy. All that is required is to assemble a critical number of believable persons to attest to the existence of the supposed threat, then to offer a solution to the "crisis" thus created. Interestingly enough, the suggested solution often has little to do with the threat. It is also notable that factual lies are often involved, but are repeated frequently enough and by enough people that they assume the patina of truth. Examples? "CO_2 is the worst greenhouse gas." (It's not. Water vapor accounts for nearly 86% of the greenhouse effect. Do you want to try to eliminate water vapor?) "Nuclear energy is the most dangerous power source." (Actually, it's the safest, even counting Chernobyl, which was designed as a plutonium generator rather than purely a power source.) "Private enterprise has failed to give us affordable health care – we need the government to regulate it." (Almost all of the problems with health care arise from the government interference that already exists.) People and the media will argue endlessly against such factual corrections, such is the power of repeated lies. Eventually the lies become so widely accepted that government supports them and enshrines them in legislation. This is the technique of 'the big lie', attributed to Herr Goebbles, Hitler's propaganda minister.

Fear tactics such as the above are originated and stoked for purposes quite removed from the allegations made. Those who wish to bring industrialized nations down to the level of second or third world countries in the name of "equity" push the greenhouse campaign against CO_2. The oil and coal companies have funded and supported organizations such as Greenpeace and the Sierra Club in the fight against nuclear power, using them as pawns (witting or unwitting) against the intrinsically cheaper nuclear power that threatens their hegemony. Insurance companies have lobbied for government supported employer insurance, arguing against any thought that they might need to appeal to each individual and tailor a policy to that person's particular needs.

The use of fear tactics by politicians is a clear indication of a hidden agenda.

A simple cure for the practice of fear mongering in politics would be banning from political or legislative office any person using fear tactics if the threat is eventually proven to be baseless. This would engender a commendable caution on the part of any politician tempted to shout 'fire!' in any political theater, and would remove the more blatant practitioners of the art of fright from the public arena.

We might even extend the same sanctions to the "scientists" who willingly generate and/or support such fears.

IMPROVING THE BREED

When we breed plants and animals with the intent of producing offspring with favorable characteristics, we do so by a winnowing process, removing those from the breeding pool that do not have the desirable characteristics or do not have them to the same level as others in the pool. This is not a new process; nature has been at it ever since life has existed on the planet. Nature, however, is slow and erratic, chance and circumstance being the only selectors with which Nature has to work. The reason that man can produce favorable (or what we consider favorable) results within relatively brief time periods is that we consciously direct the process.

Nobody really questions the efficiency of the selective process when we apply it to improving our dogs, corn, horses, turnips, flowers and cats, but for some reason we get queasy when the time comes to apply it to our institutions and our everyday lives. There is not too much trouble when it is applied to sports teams, at least at the semi professional or professional level, but there is some pressure against applying it to school sports. When even the suggestion that it might be applied to entrenched government or union controlled professions the objections become profound to absolute.

Much to-do is made about the generally poor quality of our educational system, but the cure is, and always has been, obvious: select out the poorest performing teachers. The weeding process need not be violent –simply removing the worst performing 2% each year would probably boost the international standing of our school system from the bottom 25% to the upper 10% within a decade. There is a secondary pressure, against any such procedure by unions, in that it would mean that the wages of the best teachers would need to be raised to compensate for the risks involved in entering the profession. This goes against the socialistic tendencies that have come into vogue amongst unions, even though such merit-based compensation would also improve the quality of the teacher feedstock.

It is unfortunate that government and unions stand foursquare against known methods of improvement. We all suffer for this.

None of this is new. We know how to improve our schools (and thereby our children and society in general), but we allow power wielded by the selfish to dictate to us a poorer existence. Perhaps placing some responsibility for this where it belongs, on such organizations as teachers unions, would bring some pressure. Why couldn't a poorly educated student sue for non-performance on the part of his or her teachers? Why should the government stand in the way of such a potentially beneficial lawsuit?

OOPS!

It is a truism that everyone makes mistakes. Mistakes however, can be corrected by thorough fact checking, editing and careful consideration. There is a class of mistakes, though, that is especially resistant to detection and correction – those that result from the action of the Law of Unintended Consequences. It is notable that this Law operates very frequently with legislation. Who could have foreseen that welfare laws would raise illegitimacy rates by 800%? That saving the pelican and eagle by banning DDT could result in the sickness of nearly a billion (and counting) human beings and the death of over 110 million, mostly children? That price controls by President Nixon could nearly destroy the prosperous U.S. plastics industry?

The chief reason that legislators routinely ignore the Law of Unintended Consequences is that the victims of the Law are insulated by time and space from the more obvious beneficiaries of whatever legislation is being generated. The victims of banning DDT were (and are) chiefly poor black Africans and the poor of India and South America, all far removed in both time and space from the initiators of the laws, who proudly point to the recovering stocks of pelicans and eagles as proof of their righteousness. Certainly each pelican or eagle alive today is worth a measly 120 or so dead Africans, especially if the media doesn't make a point of noticing them? Of course the ban saved the lives of billions of mosquitoes too.

Virtually all legislation, virtually all laws, virtually all bills generated by governments have unintended consequences. Frankly, my dear, legislators don't give a damn. In nearly all, if not all cases the victims of government actions are hidden by time, distance or both, and can thus be ignored.

More people have died, and are still dying, of malaria as a result of DDT legislation than the sum of the genocides of Hitler, Mao, Stalin, Pol Pot, the Janjaweed and the Tutsis all put together. That's an impressive record for a handful of American legislators who pushed an EPA environmental agenda to ban DDT.

Nobody can avoid the Law of Unintended Consequences, least of all politicians.

Careful and limited testing best minimizes the Law of Unintended Consequences. Any new legislation, any new law should be tried out in small scale, in a limited area. If there are questions or other objections, these too should be tested. The results of such testing should be considered before applying laws or legislation on a wider basis. After all, do we not require extensive testing before using drugs and medical devices? Additionally, of course, there should be the greatest reluctance to simply make blanket one-size-fits-all laws. For example, in the case of DDT, applying a ban selectively in areas where deleterious results were found would have been sufficient, without spreading the ban worldwide on a storm of politically driven bad science.

CREATING PROBLEMS TO MAKE WORSE

Government programs, it has been observed, take on a life of their own, becoming virtually immortal in the process. In the natural order of things, programs outlive their original intent and simply become institutionalized. At length, the problems created by these dinosaurs grow to the point that they attract additional governmental attention. This attention virtually never takes the form of abolition, but rather generates another program to "improve" the earlier program. (We can't just put all of those fine public servants out of work.)

Consider a prime example of this. During the Second World War the government mandated a freeze on wages. Meanwhile people were being drafted and were volunteering for the armed forces. This increased consumption greatly, with a coincidental decrease in productive people. (A person leaving the productive sector to become a soldier no longer produces, but becomes a major consumer. On the average a member of the military consumes 100 to 200 times as much as a worker; guns, ammunition, tanks, etc. being rather high-end items.) The freeze put manufacturers in a bind –labor was suddenly scarce and the demand for goods skyrocketed. Ordinarily companies would simply offer higher wages, but the mandate prevented this, so a government-approved alternative developed: companies offered health insurance to attract employees, and government agreed that neither the employee nor the employer would be liable for taxes on the benefits or costs of the insurance. Of course the program didn't end after the war, so today we have employer provided (really government subsidized) health insurance. Rather than tailoring policies to fit the individual purchaser, the insurance companies now tailor them to the employer, making them only an approximate fit to the consumer. The employees overuse the policies because they are "free" and the inefficiencies multiply, along with health care costs.

Now we will create a national health policy to correct these problems, increase the costs and decrease the service. This will be a great opportunity for a good capitalistic health insurance company to integrate vertically, providing health services – offshore.

There is no problem that cannot be made worse by government assistance.

There can be no better argument for the reduction of government to the absolute minimum than the repeated proof of the multiplier effect of government program piled on top of government program.

Reagan was right; there are no more terrifying words in the English language than 'I'm from the government, and I'm here to help.'

DEATH AND BODIES

In times past, the King owned everything in his kingdom, including his subjects. For a person to attempt suicide was, therefore, an attempt to destroy the King's property, and was illegal. The Church agreed with the King, and made suicide a sin, to dissuade those who might consider heaven a better residence than the misery of medieval serfdom. The prohibition against suicide exists to this day in both the Church and in governmental law.

Most of us are not fans of Dr. Kevorkian, but he made an important point; some perfectly sane and logical people make reasoned evaluations that their lives are of negative value. If law stands in the way of them ending their own lives, the law is stating, quite clearly, that they do not own themselves. Could there be anything more comprehensive, invasive and totalitarian?

The entire concept of ownership is that the thing owned is *ours*, to do with whatever we wish. If one owns, say a book, they may keep it, write in it, donate it to a library, give it to another, abuse it or destroy it because that person *owns* it. That is the very meaning of ownership. Ownership is one of the mainstays of freedom, and whenever it is restricted, we are that much less free.

Isn't it odd that many of the same persons who consider that any law against abortion is an interference with a woman's right to control her body are quick to condemn the sale of organs?

Tens of thousands die each year for lack of transplant organs. The number of donated organs is pitifully small, mainly because the government has made it illegal to sell organs, even organs to be harvested after death. This is hypocrisy of the first order, for everyone else in the chain from organ donor to patient benefits greatly. The hospital, the surgeon, the harvesting agency even the nurses all benefit, but the source, the donor (or the donor's heirs) get nothing. If someone wants to sell their usable organs after death (or before), they should be free to do so, striking the best deal that they can. People die because we are forbidden to do this. Politicians and legislators, of course, hold themselves blameless for such deaths.

If we can't own and control our own bodies, then we are truly enslaved.

Many people react to the idea of selling body parts with horror, although they will happily support the Red Cross blood drive when it comes to their neighborhood, and smile at the selfless act when a brother gives his kidney to a sibling. The argument is made that the selling of organs (before and/or after death) will result in a black market. Just the opposite is true – a black market is created by scarcity, high value and appositive legislation. A regulated market with wide availability would drop price, increase supply and save lives. There is a popular bumper sticker that goes: DON'T TAKE YOUR ORGANS TO HEAVEN. HEAVEN KNOWS WE NEED THEM   HERE. In reality, you can't take them to heaven; once you are dead they are worm food.

Striking all laws against our possession of our own bodies would be a good start. Once done, the rest follows naturally.

The patchwork approach and scarcity of organs we have now could lead to some interesting aberrations as the following story illustrates:

THE ABORTION

"BRENDA SUE?" THE NURSE LOOKED UP FROM HER CLIPBOARD AT THE SOLE OCCUPANT OF THE TASTEFULLY DECORATED WAITING ROOM.

"YES, MA'M, I'M BRENDA," THE VERY PREGNANT WOMAN STOOD UP.

"MY NAME IS ANN. FOLLOW ME, PLEASE. DOCTOR MORRISON WILL SEE YOU NOW. RIGHT THIS WAY," THE NURSE MOTIONED BRENDA DOWN A SHORT HALL AND INTO A COMFORTABLE OFFICE, WHERE SHE SEATED HER IN A PLUSH ARMCHAIR.

"MA'M," BRENDA LOOKED UP AT ANN, "I AIN'T GOT MUCH MONEY. I'M ON AFDC AND WELFARE --"

ANN LAID A HAND ON BRENDA'S SHOULDER. "DON'T WORRY ABOUT IT. THERE'S NO CHARGE TO YOU FOR ANYTHING THAT WE DO. ALL OF OUR FUNDING COMES FROM OTHER SOURCES." SHE TURNED AND LEFT, CLOSING THE DOOR SOFTLY BEHIND HER. A MOMENT LATER, THE DOOR OPENED AND A KINDLY FACED CHUBBY MAN ENTERED, WEARING A WHITE COAT BEARING THE NAMETAG 'DR. MORRISON'. "NO, NO. DON'T GET UP. THAT ARMCHAIR SUCKS YOU RIGHT IN, AND IT'S HARD ENOUGH JUST STANDING UP WHEN YOU'RE PREGNANT." HE STEPPED FORWARD AND SHOOK BRENDA'S HAND, THEN RETREATED BEHIND HIS DESK. "WHAT CAN I DO FOR YOU TODAY, BRENDA?"

BRENDA LOOKED DOWN AT HER SWOLLEN BELLY. "WELL - AH - THE CLINIC DOWN THE STREET SAID THAT THEY COULDN'T DO AN ABORTION, BECAUSE I WAS TOO FAR ALONG, AND I SAW YOUR

SIGN, AND I THOUGHT - -." SHE SNIFFED. "MAYBE I COULD GET A POS — AH A POSARM - -."

"A POSTPARTUM ABORTION?" DR MORRISON ASKED HELPFULLY.

"YEAH, ONE OF THOSE," SHE AFFIRMED WITH A NOD.

"I SEE. WELL, IT'S CERTAINLY AN OPTION, ALWAYS IS, YOU KNOW, ALWAYS IS. THAT'S WHY WE'RE HERE. I'LL HAVE TO ASK YOU A FEW QUESTIONS, OF COURSE, AND YOU'LL HAVE TO SIGN A FEW PAPERS. ALWAYS HAVE TO DO THE PAPERWORK, YOU KNOW," HE SMILED, A KINDLY, CHERUBIC SMILE.

BRENDA SMILED AND NODDED IN RETURN. "SURE, I KNOW ALL ABOUT PAPERWORK. AFDC PEOPLE ARE ALWAYS HAVING ME SIGN STUFF. I DON'T MIND."

DR. MORRISON NODDED AND TURNED ON THE COMPUTER THAT OCCUPIED THE CENTER OF HIS DESK. A SCREEN IN THE CORNER OF THE DESK CAME ALIGHT WITH A DOCUMENT. "COULD I ASK HOW FAR ALONG YOU ARE WITH YOUR PREGNANCY?"

SHE NODDED. "A BIT OVER EIGHT MONTHS. MY OLD BOYFRIEND MADE ME PREGNANT THEN LEFT ME WHEN HE FOUND OUT, AND MY NEW BOYFRIEND DON'T WANT NO KID AROUND."

"YOU DIDN'T USE ANY BIRTH CONTROL? PILLS, CONDOMS, DIAPHRAGM?"

"NAH. MY BOYFRIEND DIDN'T LIKE THEM RUBBER THINGS, AND THE PILLS COST TWENTY, TWENTY-FIVE BUCKS A MONTH. BESIDES I FIGGERED A KID WOULD HELP ME KEEP HIM AROUND. HE ALWAYS SAID THAT HE LIKED KIDS."

Dr. Morrison typed briefly. "I see. Have you considered adoption?"

Brenda shook her head. "No way. My Ma always told me about how it hurts to have a kid, and then just give it away? No." She suddenly looked concerned. "It doesn't hurt, does it? I mean what you do?"

"No, no, of course not. You will be most comfortable before and during the procedure. Never know what is happening, as a matter of fact. And, of course, no pain afterward."

"Good. I don't like pain."

Dr. Morrison nodded. "Now, what disposition do you want of the body? I might suggest that an organ donation program would be an excellent choice. You could actually help others and possibly save a life."

Brenda gaped at the Doctor for a moment, then brightened. "Why, I never thought of that! Sure, why not help someone when I can? I suppose it just goes to waste otherwise." She hesitated. "It don't go to no medical school or anything does it?"

"Oh, absolutely not. Body parts are far too precious for that." Dr. Morrison typed briefly, pressed the 'print' button, and a few neatly typed sheets slid out of the printer. "You sign here, saying that you are requesting this procedure of your own free will, and here, for your wishes for disposition of the body," he pointed with his

PEN, AND OFFERED THE INSTRUMENT TO HER. "THEN PRESS YOUR RIGHT THUMB IN THE SQUARE AT THE BOTTOM OF EACH PAGE. THE FINGERPRINT ASSURES ANYONE ASKING THAT IT IS INDEED YOU WHO SIGNED, NOT SOME STRANGER."

BRENDA DID AS SHE WAS DIRECTED, THEN LOOKED UP. "WHEN CAN YOU DO IT?" SHE ASKED.

"WHY, RIGHT AWAY," DR. MORRISON ASSURED. "DID YOU WANT TO WAIT? WE CAN DO IT ANY TIME THAT YOU WANT."

"NO, THE SOONER THE BETTER. MY NEW BOYFRIEND DON'T LIKE THE IDEA OF A BABY. ME NEITHER."

"NURSE," DR. MORRISON CALLED, AND ANN, WHO HAD USHERED BRENDA INTO THE ROOM EARLIER, APPEARED AT THE DOOR. "PLEASE PREPARE BRENDA FOR THE PROCEDURE, ALERT DR. HENDERSON FOR THE ANESTHESIA, THEN SEE TO THE FILING OF THESE PAPERS. HAVE TO KEEP ALL THE PAPERWORK LEGAL, YOU KNOW."

THE NURSE NODDED AND BECKONED BRENDA OUT OF THE ROOM. "TAKE OFF YOUR CLOTHES, PUT THIS ON AND HAVE A SEAT ON THE END OF THE TABLE THERE. DOCTOR HENDERSON WILL BE HERE IN JUST A MOMENT"

***

DR. MORRISON LEANED BACK IN HIS CHAIR AND SMILED AT ANN. "SO WHAT ARE THE RESULTS OF BRENDA'S PROCEDURE?"

ANN SHUFFLED A FEW PAPERS. "BLOOD WENT TO THE BLOOD BANK, OF COURSE, BOTH EYES WERE TAKEN, LIVER WAS A PERFECT MATCH TO A RECIPIENT, PROBABLY WON'T EVEN NEED ANTI-

REJECTION DRUGS, HEART, BOTH LUNGS, BOTH KIDNEYS, MOST OF THE BONE AND SOME OF THE SKIN FOUND RECIPIENTS. ALL THE CORD BLOOD IS BEING PROCESSED FOR STEM CELLS. BRENDA PROBABLY SAVED FOUR LIVES TODAY." SHE SMILED SADLY. "SHE WAS A SCHOOL DROPOUT. DO YOU EVER THINK THAT ALL THIS DEPENDS ON IGNORANCE OF THE ENGLISH LANGUAGE?"

"ALL THE TIME," DR. MORRISON ASSURED HER. "HOW ABOUT THE BABY?"

"IN NEONATAL CARE FOR A WEEK OR TWO, WE ALREADY HAVE A GOOD HOME PICKED OUT." SHE HESITATED. "I GUESS IGNORANCE IS IMPORTANT, BUT BEING IN A STATE THAT ALLOWS DOCTOR ASSISTED SUICIDE IS EVEN MORE IMPORTANT."

DR. MORRISON NODDED. "YES, THERE'S THAT, TOO."

~~~~~~~~~~~

SUBSIDIES

While it is widely understood that government lives by thievery, there is a certain practice that compounds the crime in a manner not practiced by any sensible thief. This is the practice of subsidies.

In a subsidy, the legislator(s) direct a certain portion of monies taken from taxpayers into the hands of other persons or corporations. This action is always taken as a result of money, influence or support being returned to the legislators or their party. Sometimes the subsidy takes the form of laws, tariffs, price supports, legislated minimum prices, minimum wages or other favorable treatment rather than cash. (Money has the undesirable stigma of being easily comprehended by the average citizen, unlike more arcane legislative acts.)

Unfortunately, the evil does not end with the money or favorable treatment, for the existence of such governmental largess in the hands of the favored business or person acts as an impediment to that business's competitors. Thus it is that we have corn syrup sweeteners in our foods rather than natural sugar, the import of (much cheaper and healthier) sugar being heavily discouraged by a high tariff, causing

U.S. sugar prices to be about three times that of other places in the world. As a result, candy makers have virtually all moved out of the country, taking thousands of jobs with them. Europe sells its heavily subsidized Airbus at an artificially low price in competition to Boeing. The price differential is so large that even the military, charged with protection of the country, wanted to buy the European aircraft. In this manner, not only does the taxpayer get to pay the subsidy, but also gets to pay the higher price engendered by lack of competition.

The practice of subsidy, by either money or favorable legislation destroys jobs, wastes money, harms consumers and only benefits selected businesses and certain legislators. It is the antithesis of free enterprise and a capitalistic economy.

A subsidy is the result of a bribe given to one or more legislators; it should decorate them like Hester Prynne's scarlet letter, but with less integrity.

The whole concept of a subsidy is based on two concepts: the government is a strong-arm thief and the government can play favorites. A subsidy benefits a few at the expense of the many. It has no economic, moral or logical justification and should be eliminated and made illegal.

The proper response to another country subsidizing one or another industry would be for the buyer to purchase the entire amount of the subsidized product, corner the market, raise the price and resell it. The taxpayers who subsidize the product will quickly get tired of giving the buyer free money.

THE ZERO SUM GAME

The concept of a "zero sum game" can be illustrated by the game of penny-stack. In penny-stack, two persons each stack up a number of pennies. One person is 'even', the other 'odd'. If the top coin in each stack is the same, 'even' takes both, if different, 'odd' takes both. The game continues until both stacks are exhausted, whereupon the coins are restacked and the game continued. Regardless of how long the game is played, there are always the same total number of pennies at the end as there were in the beginning, thus it is a "zero sum" game, even though one person may have won all of the pennies. Virtually all gambling games are zero-sum games. House (as in casino) gambling games are negative-sum games.

A large percentage of people regard the entire world as a zero sum game; they conceive of wealth as being limited, much like the number of pennies in the game of penny-stack. In reality, of course, wealth is created through human effort, and the total amount of wealth is always being increased. This fact is obvious on the surface – just consider how much wealthier the world is now than a hundred years ago. Still, many people act on the assumption that there is a fixed amount of wealth in the world, leading to the impression that the existence of wealthy and poor people is evidence of some unfair scheme of wealth distribution. This outlook leads to the idea that those who have should give to those who have not, the essential concept behind communism and socialism, ignoring the fact that wealth is created through human effort, and that human effort is inherently unequal. Politicians buy into the fixed wealth concept very easily because they continually operate on the principle of moving wealth from those who have it to others, thereby buying power and contributions from those whom they favor. Politicians operate governments.

Since governments do not produce, governmental actions are at most zero sum games. Many are negative sum games.

The fact that governmental actions are inherently zero-sum or negative-sum should be a concept driven home to all of our legislators and politicians as well as citizens. In the free market, a person's labor produces more than what that laborer is paid, but in the zero-sum game of government, this is not true. It is impossible for any governmental program to either create more jobs than it destroys, make more wealth than it creates, or to save money. They can only make jobs by destroying other jobs or get wealth through theft. The truth of the matter is that governmental programs, at their best, hold place, but most simply waste money, destroy wealth and strangle initiative. Neither wealth nor jobs can be created by stealing them from one person then giving them to another, especially if there is a 30% commission.

SOLAR

The "green revolution", which is neither green nor a revolution, is enamored of solar power. There are three basic types of solar power. The one devised by nature, chlorophyll, is quite inefficient at about 5% conversion of sunlight. Heat converters are 25% to 40% efficient. A good photovoltaic solar panel has a conversion efficiency of about 35%. There are nanotechnology solar panels under development that promise efficiencies of 60% to 75 %. The best place to situate solar panels, of course is in desert areas, where there is plenty of sunlight, little cloud cover and lots of land with minimal value to man or wildlife. The solar power available in America's Southwestern badlands is plentiful enough to supply all of the country's energy needs four to five times over. There is only one catch:

When the sun doesn't glow,

The electricity doesn't flow.

At best that means we somehow need to store the daytime power to tide us over the night and, more importantly, over a few extended periods of bad weather.

Storage schemes currently run to reservoirs of chemicals that can store and release energy as heat. These are rather inefficient. An added problem arises inasmuch as most civilized areas avoid deserts and are hence remote from the source of solar power, and transmission losses also add to the inefficiencies. There is one interesting suggestion that the electricity be used to produce hydrogen, which in turn could be used, with very high efficiency, to work in fuel cells. Fuel cell technology, although currently expensive, is compact enough to power automobiles, but hydrogen storage is currently difficult and bulky. In short, we can produce electricity from the sun, our cost/price ratio is improving rapidly, although it is still higher than all other commercial systems, but we have no way to economically use the energy. This has resulted from a lopsided governmental encouragement of solar power without consideration of the inevitable downstream problems. This would not have occurred if market forces had shaped development, for commercial developments are always conscious of practical (read profitable) considerations.

Government "planning" is too subject to outside considerations, mostly donations of money or influence.

Government interference with technological innovation creates stumbling blocks. The best function for government in developing desired technology is to point and say: "There is the goal! Here is the prize!" then stand back. What would the space program look like today if Kennedy, instead of establishing a government program, had said; "There's the moon. First ones to establish a self-sustaining colony there will own it."?

~~~~~~~~~~~~~~~~

CLOUDY WEATHER

NIGHT WAS STARTING TO MOVE IN AND THE HOUSE COMPUTER DECIDED THAT IT WAS TIME TO SWITCH TO BATTERY POWER. THE MAIN LIGHTS WENT OFF, THE LED LIGHTING CAME ON, THE STOVE, MICROWAVE AND AIR CONDITIONING/HEATING ALL LOCKED DOWN. THE REFRIGERATOR AND FREEZER SWITCHED OVER TO THE HOLDING PLATES, THE NO-ACCESS LOCK ON THE FREEZER ACTIVATING AT THE SAME TIME.

JUNE HAD TAKEN OUT THE INGREDIENTS FOR THE EVENING MEAL WELL BEFORE THE STOVE HAD LOCKED DOWN, AND DINNER WAS KEEPING WARM IN AN INSULATED POT. WINTERTIME WAS ALWAYS A RACE BETWEEN GETTING HOME AND GETTING DINNER BEFORE DARK. BATTERY POWER JUST WASN'T SUFFICIENT FOR THE HEAVY LOADS OF ELECTRIC MOTORS AND STOVES. SHE TURNED ON THE TV AND SETTLED DOWN TO WAIT FOR JIM, HER HUSBAND, THEIR THREE KIDS AND TO CATCH UP ON THE DAY'S NEWS.

DINNER WAS A NOISY AFFAIR, JUNE TRYING TO TALK WITH JIM OVER THE EXITED JABBER OF THE THREE KIDS AND THE DRONE OF THE TV IN THE BACKGROUND. SUDDENLY THE NOISE VOLUME UNDERWENT A SHARP INCREASE AS ALL THREE KIDS STARTED CHEERING. "NO SCHOOL TOMORROW! WE'RE CLOSED."

JUNE TURNED TO LOOK AT THE TV, WHERE A LIST OF SCHOOL CLOSINGS WAS SCROLLING UP THE SCREEN. "OH NO," SHE GROANED. "CLOUDS AND RAIN IN THE DESERT. ONLY NECESSESARY UTILITIES ARE ON, RESIDENTIAL POWER IS OFF, SOLAR COLLECTORS ARE GOING TO BE AT ONE-

QUARTER POWER. YOU KNOW WHAT THIS MEANS?"
SHE TURNED TO JIM.

"SURE, I STAY HOME TOMORROW. SLEEP IN.
WE CUDDLE UP TO KEEP WARM. EAT CANNED
GOODS. GET SOME CHORES DONE AROUND HERE."

JUNE SHOOK HER HEAD. "I MEAN RAIN IN THE
DESERT HAS ONLY HAPPENED THREE TIMES SINCE
WE'VE BEEN MARRIED."

~~~~~~~~~~~~~~

ELITES

There always seems to be those persons in any group who think extra-well of themselves, who feel that somehow they are better than others. The superiority feelings of these persons may arise from almost any source, from education to skills or simply by having passed through the vaginas of special parents. Politics seems to be a favorite occupation of such, for it offers an opportunity to confirm their conceits while exempting them from the hurly-burly of making a living by being actively productive. It should be noted that persons who delegate to themselves these elevated (at least in their own minds) positions often labor mightily but produce little of value. Indeed, they often produce negative wealth or become divisive of common productivity. People who consider themselves superior should be viewed with suspicion; while it is possible that they are indeed members of a productive elite, there are fairly long odds that they are of the other sort.

The marketplace favors those who produce value, and the wealth produced therefrom is so prodigious that it can tolerate the presence of a certain number of drones and others who produce less than they consume, but this should not be construed to mean that such persons are of positive value to mankind as a whole. They are the economic system's version of bedbugs and fleas.

It is very important that we do not listen to the importunings of self- styled elites and elect them to office in any capacity. They are self-centered and, generally, selfish. These are bad traits in those who would govern us.

Free markets serve everyone, but there are those who wish everyone to serve them.

Like trying to eliminate envy, attempting to eliminate feelings of elitism is probably impossible. This does not mean that we should be socially accepting of them. This is one of those bothersome human conceits that would be best diminished by the proper application of social design, by making it as unacceptable in society as indoor smoking has been. It is of no productive value.

LAWS

Politicians being politicians and governmental systems being what they are, laws on all manner of things tend to proliferate. There is no complaint, no social ill, no human or animal injury, no transaction that is too petty to be addressed by one more law, one more legislative agenda. If there be a lack of an obvious problem, it is not beyond the capability of politicians to create one out of whole cloth, in order that it might be addressed by one more legal fart.

The evils of alcohol drew so much public attention that Progressive activists, prodding legislatures, were able to get all strong drink banned by a Constitutional amendment. This instantly created an entire new criminal class, not only of brewers and distillers, but drinkers as well. It also created a whole new set of criminal enterprises from bathtub gin to smugglers and speakeasies. Although later repealed, the effects of the amendment are with us yet in the form of criminal mobs birthed in Prohibition, in excessive taxes on alcohol and in blue laws.

Any law that addresses a behavior by punishing it or criminalizing it will, by obvious logic, create criminals out of those who practice the behavior. The banning of recreational drugs, with the exceptions of nicotine, alcohol and caffeine, has produced a huge criminal class and opened a number of profitable new criminal businesses, at great public expense, without any discernable positive results. This is the natural result of virtually all laws, although often the effects are removed in time and space.

We should ponder these facts whenever new restrictive legislation is considered. As we contemplate the current political pot stirring over the ever-changing climate of the planet we may want to take care. The world does not need organized eco-criminals.

The more laws there are, the more criminals there will be.

This simple fact makes legislators partners in the commission of crimes of various sorts. The elimination of a few laws would probably destroy billions of dollars worth of criminal enterprises, save lives and remove a large number of relatively harmless criminals from our prisons. It would also eliminate a number of expensive government programs by making them obsolete.

Great caution should be exercised by lawmakers in making restrictive laws, and the greater the arena in which those laws are to be applied, the more cautious they should be. If we make over-zealous laws about climate change, who will replace the lost wealth that will be expended in enacting their constraints? Who will stand accountable for the inevitable deaths that will result? Who will make recompense if the effects of man's doings are found to be negligible? The answer, of course, is that nobody will, least of all the legislators who are to blame.

ANOMOLIES

Legislators, being often driven by emotion (both their own and the public's) will make laws based on one particular instance, often in response to a particularly spectacular crime. Almost invariably this type of law is bad law, for the instance that produced the law is seldom repeated, but the law is subsequently stretched to cover other, more common, instances. The stretching of laws to cover wider than intended occasions effectively comprises the making of new law without any accompanying legislation or public input. For example: there are Federal and State laws against the use of a firearm in the commission of a crime. These have given rise to other laws, Federal and State, against simply possessing a firearm during the commission of a felony. These laws have been "stretched" by various court decisions to the point that simply possessing an empty cartridge during the commission of a crime is a crime of its own, a ridiculous extension, which has been created to enable prosecutors to demand greater sentences.

Laws and legislation made in response to odd and unusual occurrences address a non-existent world.

The cure for this problem is obvious –

stop making laws and passing legislation that address limited or very unusual problems; let's specify at least 100 occurrences as the minimum number of instances needed before generating a law. Generally, already existent laws can address such special problems, and where they cannot be so addressed, long and careful consideration should be given to produce laws that cover the entire genre of which the problem is only a sample. This will result in laws that are stronger and of wider application, thus resisting the impulse to stretch them. Do we actually need a law to do this? How about a little legislative calm and consideration? The roar of the emotional crowd will pass, but bad laws are forever.

INTERSTATE TRADE

The Founding Fathers thought that one function of the new government should be to regulate interstate trade, preventing states with particular resources such as minerals or conditions favorable to certain crops from using their particular natural advantages to demand extraordinary benefits from other states, or to charge fees for passage through their state on the way to another. It was probably a good idea. It is unfortunate that they did not reckon with the ability of politicians and the legal system to stretch the original idea all out of shape. In the modern era, almost all items move in interstate trade and even the most mundane items can cross state lines. The government has stretched the original intent of the law, to make "regular" the trade between states, into an excuse to interfere on the most basic level with virtually all actions, products, property and undertakings of almost every citizen of the United States.

A bit of background: During the Great Depression, the government, under FDR, decided, despite the fact that people were literally starving in the streets and soup kitchens existed in almost every city, that it would be a good idea to limit the amount of food being produced in order to keep prices on various food items high, farmers and growers being substantial supporters of the Democratic Party. Orange growers in California therefore poured kerosene on orange crops and grain farmers let fertile fields lie fallow while people starved. These agricultural policies extended into the beginnings of WWII, when the pressures of the war began to modify them.

Into this scenario, came a farmer, Roscoe Filburn, who was in the habit of growing "rough" wheat, a variety of wheat that stored well but was unsuitable for making flour, being low in gluten. It did, however make excellent chicken feed, and he fed his chickens with it, (growing this in excess of the 11 acres of ordinary wheat that the government permitted.) The Secretary of Agriculture, Wickard, sued Filburn (317 U.S. 111) on the contention that his growing of additional grain to feed his chickens (a purely local activity), affected interstate trade, since the grain that he grew deducted from the amount of wheat that *might* have been produced in another state, thus *possibly* affecting interstate commerce. The Supreme Court, under Justice Harlan Stone, upheld Wickard. Since that time, the federal government has seen fit to cram almost any desired interference with internal state affairs under the statute, from regulation of school curricula to dictating that ice cream be sold by volume, not by weight (resulting in ice cream whipped to include air, increasing the volume. Have you ever tasted real "homemade" ice cream? It weighs about a pound per pint and a cone is a meal.) The elasticity of the interstate clause in the Constitution is breathtaking. The entire Obama Health Care bill is based on the power of the Federal government to intrude on our affairs through this clause. It is the excuse that the government makes to interfere with local schools, control the amount of certain crops to be grown, regulates the price of various agricultural products, dictates truck routes and what those trucks may carry and enforces local environmental dictates.

The interstate trade clause is a breach in the wall of our sovereignty.

There is one simple cure for the problems raised by the Supreme Court decision in this case, and that is to produce a Constitutional Amendment eliminating the Interstate Clause. Nothing less will do. Simply undoing the original decision will not change the widespread fruit of this poison vine.

ALCOHOL

Uncounted centuries ago mankind discovered ethyl alcohol. Alcohol can be made from almost anything containing sugar or starch, thanks to the voracious appetite of a number of different types of yeast, which happily consume the goodies and give off alcohol as a waste product. (Look at it this way: the alcohol in your beer is essentially yeast pee.) Long after the discovery of alcoholic beverages, distillation was invented, and one of the first products of the distillation process (which is used for all sorts of chemicals such as gasoline) was alcohol. At this point it was realized that alcohol would burn, which led to flaming desserts, fire-eaters and other spectacular displays. When man's inventiveness took a turn toward the mechanical replacement of the horse however, alcohol graduated from beverage and the chafing dish to fuel for vehicles. One of the earliest cars, the renowned Stanley Steamer often used alcohol as a fuel and the German V-2 rocket employed it.

In a fast-forward to the present, alcohol has received renewed attention as a fuel in the face of the air pollution resulting from the use of petroleum-derived hydrocarbons as fuel (alcohol is also a hydrocarbon, but is not generally derived from petroleum). A few countries, blessed with ideal conditions for growing sugar cane, have seen a large portion of their automotive fuel needs met by alcohol on a fairly economical basis. Other countries, jealous of such success, have attempted imitation by using corn, potatoes, beets, switchgrass and other starchy or sugary agricultural products. Sadly, at this point, government and human greed have interacted. A number of large agricultural concerns have seen a new market for corn in the production of alcohol as a fuel. It is equally sad that alcohol is not an economically viable substitute for petroleum distillates as fuel under most conditions. This problem can be overcome handily, however, by the proper application of political contributions, causing thereby laws, subsidies and other encouragements to be distilled from the body politic.

Quite aside from the fact that governmental support of alcohol as a fuel comes from the taxpayer's pocket, there are other serious side effects. The land used to grow corn must be fertilized, a source of pollution in and of itself, the agricultural land is taken out of other possible productive use, the growing of corn consumes almost as much hydrocarbon derived gasoline or diesel as alcohol produced but, most importantly, corn is *food*. When you see that little sticker on the gas pump saying that your gas may have ten percent alcohol, understand that you are burning someone's dinner to drive yourself to the theater or to go shopping downtown.

There must be a special spot in hell for governments and politicians promoting this, at the behest of companies searching for an easier profit, in a world where millions starve to death and several billions go to bed hungry.

Political contributions are bribes. There is a good reason that bribes are considered immoral.

Have any shareholders of Archer Daniels Midland and a dozen other such companies ever stood up in a meeting and raised the issue of morality? Has anyone in the government? Of course not, because interactions between greed and government are immune to such considerations. This is one reason that political contributions should be either severely limited or, preferably, eliminated.

SUPPLY SIDE, DEMAND SIDE

Politicians love to tinker with the laws of supply and demand, mostly because they either do not understand them or do not believe in them. Unfortunately for such legislative adventurers, economic laws are much like natural laws: i.e. they are no respecter of persons or governments. The same politician who would never jump from a high building in defiance of the law of gravity will sponsor legislation that defies economic laws in the serene confidence that such laws are not only mutable but subject to the whims of man-made legalistic scribbles. Scientists and technicians who deal with natural physical laws on a daily basis understand their immutability, and concentrate on using them to their advantage. Economic laws can, likewise, be used to our advantage if they are understood. It is unfortunate that so many do not comprehend them.

The list of ills visited upon mankind by government's and politician's public display of economic ignorance, enhanced by hubris, is almost endless. The list includes war, famine, disease, depression, recessions, economic dislocation and drought, to name a few. The Second World War can, with some certainty, be laid at the feet of politicians that wanted to use economic hardship to punish their erstwhile foes, in total ignorance or disregard of the ultimate results of such economic and social pressures. Today many self-styled "economists" (mostly politicians) declare themselves "supply side" or "demand side" believers, in complete disregard of the simple truth that each of these is simply the reverse side of a two-sided coin. It is as foolish as regarding the input side of a hose as more important than the outlet side - - -one absent the other nothing will flow. Legislation that increases costs *will* increase prices, and legislation that regulates prices *will* decrease supply. The most powerful legislature, the most weasel-worded law, the cleverest lawyers, even armed forces are as powerless to change this as to change the laws of gravity.

The laws of supply and demand are more powerful than any law made by any legislature.

It would be well for all who legislate or wish to legislate to understand that economic and social laws are as unforgiving as any natural law. The fact that they are complex and as yet poorly understood does not mean that they can be ignored. Until Newton and Galileo gravity was poorly understood, but that did not make its workings one whit less real. It is time that politicians and, yes, the public at large, recognize the reality of such laws and refuse to dismiss them simply on the basis of our ignorance. Perhaps we could send those legislators who ignore such laws to special economic law classes, much as we send careless drivers to traffic schools when they ignore traffic laws.

LEGAL SLAVERY

If a person is forced to labor, against their will, for another person's benefit, that person falls into a special class of persons. The proper name for this class of persons is "slaves". The type of force used to bring about this state does not matter; it may be the whip, isolation, the chain, threats, blackmail, brain washing or a combination of two or more of these things.

Now, slavery is a long-standing institution that probably existed long before human history was recorded and has been more or less consistently with us up to and including the present time. The practice cuts across races, nationalities and geographic boundaries. Slavery can be as brutal as that practiced by the worst of seventeenth century African kings or the Incas of the Americas, or it can be as sophisticated and velvet as that practiced by the courts of the Emperors of Cathay. It is still slavery. Slavery is still practiced today, often in its more brutal forms, in some African countries and some areas of Indonesia. Much of this type of slavery is sex slavery of girls, boys and women. Some of this spills over into more enlightened countries. Enlightened countries, however, usually practice a more advanced, subtle and lucrative type of slavery.

In this advanced type of slavery the slave labors to support him (or her) self, and then yields a large portion of all earnings up to support others, the identity of the others being determined by the master of the slaves. The slave master, on the basis of favoritism, votes, cronyism and kickback donations, usually chooses those so supported. This type of slavery is particularly virulent because it captures volition itself, inasmuch as the slaves must labor for self-support and support of the their children. Those benefiting from this type of slavery are essentially slaveholders by proxy. We have managed to outsource slaveholding.

Wealth taken from one and given to another by government decree makes a slave of the loser, a slave trader of the government and a slaveholder of the recipient.

One of the phrases popular in the 1960s was "wage slave", borrowed from the followers of Marx. It is unfortunate that there is somewhat more than a grain of truth in the phrase, although not in the sense that those with communistic (or communal) leanings meant it.

An employee who works for a wage does so under a contract, either written or understood, and exchanges his or her efforts for money and/or other benefits. This is an honorable agreement, and the money is a witness to the contract and performance. When the government forces itself between the parties to the contract and siphons money from one or the other as a permission for the existence of the contract, it becomes a thief of the labor and time represented by that money, making an involuntary slave of one or both parties. This is a strong reason for government to always return value for any tax, and for making such a tax both explicit and voluntary.

LIBERTY

If you decide that you will pick up and move from California to, say, Alabama, you may do so. You don't even have to tell anyone that you are doing so if you do not wish to. If you are employed, you are free to tell your employer goodbye for whatever reason or for no reason at all. If you want to throw a party and invite your friends you may do so and they are free to come or not as they see fit. You can spend your money pretty much as you wish on whatever thing that you want, and you may voice your opinion to friends around the water cooler or elsewhere with minimum risk of approbation. If you are of a literary bent, you may even write to the local newspaper and have your letter published for all to see.

Some sixty percent of the world's population cannot indulge themselves in one or more of the above acts. In many places travel must be approved, is limited and must be accompanied by "papers", official permission slips for adults. In some countries the occupation of entire classes of persons is predetermined, fixed and unalterable; in others employment is subject to governmental control and cannot be moved without ponderous effort and much accompanying suspicion. In many, any word spoken against the government or in favor of an unapproved opinion can result in incarceration, physical punishment or even death; even more so if the opinion were to be published.

People that had a new continent open to them for exploration and settlement founded this country, and the freedoms engendered by that environment were reflected in the Constitution. The freedom of the frontier settled itself into the bones and the mores of this country's inhabitants. It was difficult to enforce unreasonable laws when empty lands to the West provided a difficult but attainable refuge; the Western frontier was even a steady drain on the slavery of the South.

As the country became more settled, a steady governmental erosion of these freedoms began to take place, and that erosion is continuing, even today, at an accelerated rate. This is a dangerous trend that is stealing away our birthright the way termites steal away a house.

It is easy to assume that liberty is the normal state of affairs if you have never had it taken away from you.

Personal liberty and freedom were the founding birthright of this nation, and have accounted, in large part, for its stature in the world as well as for its great prosperity. We attempted to enshrine these freedoms in our Constitution, and for almost a century it worked, but there was a steady loss, which accelerated with Federalism, then accelerated again with Progressivism. Today this erosion is a landslide, and those who are minimally aware of it are often happy, in their unenlightened ignorance, to advance it, believing that the destruction of their vaguely understood rights is going to somehow make them safer, richer, happier and freer. Education is badly needed so that people at large are aware of the relationship between rights, freedom and independence.

PIDDELING WITH PRICES

There is probably no myth that is so pervasive and with such a hold on the minds of the thoughtless and economically uneducated public as the idea that government (and by extension politicians) can or do control and dictate prices. Acting to effectuate the myth, politicians from time to time legislate price controls on this or that thing or, sometimes, on a whole bunch of things. The results of such controls are as predictable as summer rains in Indianapolis. Politicians, naturally, profit from the imposition of price controls through a boost in their poll ratings and public approval. For some reason, probably lack of public education and a substantial time lag between application and result, people seldom connect the ensuing shortages with the legislation.

The classic example, of course, is rent controls in New York. These created a gradually growing class of slums as landlords found it unprofitable to maintain their properties and destroyed a building industry that would normally have produced new housing. An unfortunate side effect of this was that controls became almost impossible to remove due to political pressure from apartment dwellers who did not want to see their low rents soar to levels determined by a free market.

President Nixon attempted a round of price controls affecting a wide range of products. One of these was raw plastic materials, a side product of the petroleum industry, that fed a prosperous and growing plastics molding industry in the United States. The US had a pretty effective lock on new plastics technology at the time and supplied a large portion of the world's plastic needs. A year passed and the worldwide price of raw plastic crept upwards until, one by one, various types of plastic raw materials became too expensive to be legally sold in the US. In some cases the black-market price on some raw plastics exceeded the price of finished plastic products by factors of three to four times. Desperate manufacturers, in need of plastic products, turned to overseas markets, notably China, where they found a warm reception.

It was a one-way trip. The results are with us today, printed on every plastic toy, cheap plastic disposable or plastic case: '*Made in China.*'

Price controls are just a way to get public approval of killing businesses.

Price controls, like assassination, should be banned behavior for all politicians, and any suggestions in that direction should be met with general disapproval and a deep suspicion of the motives and/or education of anyone proposing them. Like a subsidy, they inhibit trade, destroy jobs and decrease general wealth. Pressure from the Fed (it is one of the financial manipulations in which the Fed engages to our detriment) should not be an excuse.

~~~~~~~~

THE VOTE

"WELL, FOR SURE, I'M GOING TO VOTE FOR CONNORS," MARY SAID. "I MEAN LOOK WHAT INFLATION'S DOING, PRICES GOING UP LIKE MAD EVERYWHERE YOU LOOK. I WAS DOWN TO THE GROCERY STORE YESTERDAY, NEEDED SOME COOKING OIL. THE PRICE ON A QUART OF OIL IS UP NEARLY A DOLLAR!"

SARAH NODDED. THE MORNING COFFEE KLATCH WAS ONE OF HER CHIEF SOURCES OF INFORMATION ON A WIDE VARIETY OF SUBJECTS BOTH NATIONAL AND NEIGHBORHOOD. "WHY CONNORS? I KINDA LIKE SCHARBER. HE'S CUTE."

"SURE," MARY ALLOWED, "HE'S A LOT CUTER THAN CONNORS, BUT CONNORS IS THE ONE THAT MAKES SENSE. HE'S GOING TO FREEZE PRICES, PUT AN END TO INFLATION. I DON'T SEE WHY THOSE GREEDY BUSINESSPEOPLE SHOULD BE ALLOWED TO JUST CHARGE MORE AND MORE FOR THE SAME THING."

SARAH CONTEMPLATED THAT FOR A MINUTE. "YEAH, THAT DOES MAKE SENSE. IT'S HARD ENOUGH TO MAKE ENDS MEET AS IT IS. YOU TALK ABOUT COOKING OIL, HAVE YOU SEEN WHAT DIAPERS ARE GOING FOR NOW?" EVERY MEMBER OF THE COFFEE KLATCH NODDED AGREEMENT. "MY HUBBY DOESN'T USUALLY VOTE, BUT I'M GOING TO GET HIM TO THE POLLS THIS TIME. CONNORS SOUNDS LIKE THE BEST BET."

***

PETERSON SAT BACK IN HIS SWIVEL CHAIR, A FILE THAT JERRY, HIS SALES MANAGER, HAD PRESENTED HIM WITH, CLUTCHED IN HIS HAND. "WE

CAN'T HOLD THE PRICE LINE, I DON'T CARE WHAT CONNORS' DAMN FOOL PRICE GUIDELINES SAY. OUR OIL FEEDSTOCK IS UP, WAGES ARE UP, ELECTRICITY IS UP. OUR COST IS $107 PER HUNDREDWEIGHT; WE CAN'T SELL AT $105, WE'LL GO BROKE."

"OBVIOUSLY," JERRY AGREED. THAT'S WHY I SAY WE DUMP THE LOCAL MARKET. IF WE CAN'T GET A GOOD PRICE ON COOKING OIL IN THE U.S., WELL, CHINA IS PAYING $122 A HUNDREDWEIGHT, TRANSPORTATION IS $9 PER HUNDREDWEIGHT, WE MAKE A REASONABLE PROFIT."

PETERSON LOOKED LIKE HE HAD JUST BIT INTO A LEMON. "WE'VE PRODUCED COOKING OIL FOR FIFTY-TWO YEARS AND ALWAYS FOUND A GOOD MARKET HERE. WE'RE AN AMERICAN COMPANY."

JERRY SHRUGGED. "WE DON'T SELL AT SOME KIND OF PROFIT, WE WON'T BE ANY KIND OF COMPANY."

PETERSON NODDED. "LET'S DO IT. HOW MUCH WILL THEY TAKE?"

JERRY STOOD UP. "ALL OF IT, AND IF WE PUT ON AN EXTRA SHIFT, THEY'LL TAKE MORE."

***

"I JUST DON'T UNDERSTAND IT," SARAH COMPLAINED. "I WANTED TO GET SOME COOKING OIL YESTERDAY, BUT THE STORE WAS OUT. IN FACT IT'S GETTING HARD TO GET ALL KINDS OF THINGS. THEY WERE ALL OUT OF 20 SIZE DIAPERS, SO I GOT THE BIGGER ONES. THEY KEEP FALLING OFF. AT LEAST THE PRICE ON DIAPERS HASN'T GONE UP."

MARY NODDED. "I WAS READING ABOUT THAT. IT'S THOSE GREEDY

MANUFACTURERS. THEY'RE SELLING ALL THAT COOKING OIL TO CHINA. THEY NEED TO MAKE A LAW TO PREVENT THAT."

~~~~~~~~~~~~~~

FOREIGN AID

The history of foreign aid stretches back into the mists of time. It was well established in Biblical times and has been practiced in many forms right on up to the present time. Generally speaking, it seldom works as advertised.

The one shining example of foreign aid that did work, the Marshall Plan after WWII is frequently cited as emblematic of all aid. The facts, however, belie this. Modern examples, along with other historical examples, show that such transfers of wealth go to the members of government and only a small amount trickles down to the populace who, the donors fondly believe, are the recipients. This process, of course, rewards the corrupt recipient governments, enhances their power and their hold on their subjects.

The effects of foreign aid are even more egregious than this, however, for the governments (and politicians) on both ends of the aid benefit, and realize that the aid exists because their citizens are poor and their countries undeveloped. This is a positive incentive for those leaders to keep their countries poor and undeveloped and to impoverish them even further by restricting foreign investment and by imposing governmental controls on various entrepreneurial activities in their country. This is why foreign aid virtually never works as intended and usually makes the recipient country worse off. Countries like Zimbabwe are more typical of the course of foreign aid. There a corrupt government has accepted aid both direct and in the form of (unrepaid) loans, while the condition of the citizens has gone from poor to bad to abysmal. Meanwhile, the monies, goods or other aid being sent are extracted from the economies of the givers, to their detriment.

The basic reason that the Marshall Plan worked and most aid fails is that the Marshall Plan help went to societies which understood the constraints of civilization, had skills and knowledge of how to use the aid and were, in large part, free of the corruption that characterizes such a huge majority of "third world" countries. Essentially they were just rebuilding an infrastructure. They used the aid to become productive, put their citizens to work and produced goods for themselves and for export, becoming prosperous in the process.

Proper foreign aid consists of providing a market for the products of a country's people.

Foreign aid of all sorts should be infrequent, minimal, short lived and entered into with great care and misgiving. This extends to all types of foreign aid, not just monetary grants. The US supports a very large, expensively equipped military, a fairly large portion of which is used to protect a number of nations that are perfectly capable of protecting themselves. This is one type of expensive foreign aid that has corrupted the recipients in a subtle way – they have become as dependent on it as any welfare queen and feel that it is their due.

The fact that there is an almost inexhaustible amount of patronage for politicians on both sides in the arrangement has made it almost unassailable. Real national power in a time of cruise missiles, nuclear warships and ICBMs does not lie in armies nearly as much as it does in productive markets. Monies spent gifting other nations should be used for shaping the home country into an economic powerhouse.

MESSING WITH MONEY

Politicians and, of course, thereby governments, love to spend money. It buys the things dear to the political heart: power, votes and personal wealth. There are only two sources from which governments can gain money; to remove it by various taxations or to print it if they have the power of coinage, which virtually all governments reserve unto themselves, although ours eschewed that for a century. Most governments do both.

There are limits to taxation: on one hand, as people are allergic to yielding large portions of their hard-earned wealth to be spent by and for others, on the other as taxation inevitably depresses prosperity, thereby decreasing the taxable base. The printing of money, however, is largely invisible to the public eye and the effects are, if it is carefully controlled, slow to be seen. From the time the present dollar was created to now, the value has fallen to 4.6% of its original worth. For all its stealth, however, monetization has real long-term effects that are debilitating on the economy and injurious to the country's citizens. Ultimately these manipulations will become fatal. In the Weimar Republic of Germany, after WWI, inflation became so bad and money so worthless that one-million mark notes were only printed on one side *in order to save ink and printing press time.*

The apparent value of money is mostly dependent on three factors: the amount of money in circulation, the speed of circulation and the amount of available, desirable goods. (This simplifies the matter substantially but is essentially true.)

The government, through the Fed, can control, to some extent, the amount of money in circulation by printing more or less or by removing some, as well as setting bank reserves. It is very difficult to remove money from circulation, as removing money from circulation generally involves high interest rates, but it is very easy to print more. The monetary inflation that Jimmy Carter delt with was somewhat less than 13%, and for two years the attempt to remove that money from circulation increased the interest rates into double digits.

The speed of circulation is very much dependent on psychological factors, such as salesmanship, fads, recessions, value perception and the shifting tides of consumerism. This is often referred to as 'consumer spending' and is urged during recessionary periods.

The amount of available goods, or at least the amount of *desirable* available goods is a complex function, but as certain goods become scarce, their perceived value rises, and thereby their price. The reverse is also true. This is sometimes exacerbated during periods of economic uncertainty by shifts in buying patterns, away from major purchases during recessionary times and toward them in inflationary times.

All of these factors add up to an overall market perception on the value of money. If the value remains relatively stable, people and businesses feel comfortable saving money, investing to obtain future earnings, making long-term contracts and in borrowing money. If the value varies, all of these things are affected. When the value of money steadily declines it is termed inflation.

Inflation is a friend of the politician – it reduces governmental debt and enables the government to print and spend more money. Slow inflation is, to the citizens, like bleeding from an anesthetized cut: slow, painless and debilitating.

Inflation is a tax on investment, jobs and prosperity.

Determination of the value of money is not difficult and it can be done roughly by comparing it to any fairly stable item. Gold is a favorite, but almost anything will work; a good quality suit, a ton of iron ore, even a haircut. Those who survey the economic scene regularly do this, referencing things to "constant dollars" pegged to one year or another. Thus we may hear of a reference to current expenditures in "1980 dollars". The difference between those 1980 dollars and the dollar today is a measure of the mismanagement of coinage by the government during the last thirty years and should be widely advertised as such. Perhaps it should be one of the 'leading economic indicators'.

It should be a primary task of the government to see that 1980 dollars are of the same value as today's or any other day's dollars. If we were to do this, as a country, our growth and prosperity would eclipse all other country's records, including our own.

DICTATORS

Tyranny is a condition, oddly enough, that people enter into willingly and often insist on maintaining. By and large, the German populace was enthusiastic about having the tyrannical socialist government of Hitler at the helm of post WW I Germany, even as he drove the country into war. They even generally approved of his intolerant racist fantasies and steadfastly ignored or blinded themselves to its uglier aspects. Incredibly, there are even people today who generally approve of his policies and economic principles.

The ability of dictators to arrive at their respective pinnacles of power is mostly due neither any great wisdom on their part, nor to any great political acumen. It is, rather, the lack of thoughtful consideration of the facts by the population at large. Not only ignorance but also the absence of even a cursory consideration of facts by people enables the dictator to attain and maintain his position. Emotions, aroused by oratory and mob appeal, are the stuff of which political power can be created. The wise dictator, then, will maintain a propaganda agency to bombard the population with the desired party line, repeating it frequently enough and loudly enough to make people believe that the propaganda indeed represents their own thinking processes. This engenders belief, belief produces conviction, which captures volition itself. The first link in establishing this type of propagandistic control is to manage and subvert the educational system, making it dependent on monies from the government. We should study carefully the history of Austria during the period that Germany was in the process of digesting it (1935-1940). It is illuminative of our times.

What great luck it is for tyrants that most people do not think. (Adolph Hitler)

It has been observed again and again that education in matters both political and financial is beneficial to the political well being of the country. When people believe that one politician or another will give them benefits or even cold cash if elected, and these people *vote*, it can be easily surmised that we are in for a world of trouble. The levers of government, the power and the structure exist quite independently of political parties and the people who may be at the titular head of the system. These can be used by dictators and tyrants quite as handily as by any others. All that is needed is to elect them to office.

Ignorant and uneducated people are good slave material. Southern slaveholders recognized this and made it a criminal offense to teach a slave to read. Anyone who graduates from any school should have a corresponding knowledge of the political structure, have read (and understood) the Constitution and demonstrate a reasonable understanding of propaganda and the role played by emotions and rhetoric in the political arena.

S.S.

Franklin Delano Roosevelt signed Social Security into law August 14, 1935. In crafting the Social Security legislation, both Congress and President Roosevelt were influenced by a general admiration in both America, and especially England, for the Italian ruler, Benito Mussolini and his social programs. Although warned of the probable long-term results of such a program by economists, the legislation sailed through Congress and across the President's desk with a minimum of political opposition. The first beneficiary was Ernest Ackerman in 1937, who received a lump sum payout. The amount of the payout was 17 cents.

As of 2010, the Social Security program has an unfunded balance of obligations in excess of 18 trillion dollars, with a measly 24 million in actual trust funds. The total the system has paid out to date has been about 11 trillion. The terms and payments of Social Security are subject to the whims and legislative political tides that control 535 Congressional members. The terms of the "contract" have been unilaterally changed by these legislators a number of times; it went from voluntary to enforced, from 1% of the first $1400 of annual incomes to 7.65% (plus 7.6% from the employer) of up to $125,000, payments went from being tax deductible to taxed, went from being a trust fund to being in the general fund, went from payments not being taxable to having 85% of the payments taxable. Would anyone with any common sense enter into any contract with terms that could be so changed unilaterally by one of the parties? Would you buy an insurance policy so written? At present, Social Security payments represent a bit more than 23% of the government budget.

There have been several propositions set forth that would transfer the Social Security system over to a commercial investment body, but, despite the fact that such an insurance fund would pay substantially greater returns than the government program, it has met with implacable political resistance. The standard argument against such a move is that the stock and bond market is risky, and that the payout amounts will be subject to market ups and downs. The real reason for the opposition is much more basic: politicians will never willingly give up such enormous amounts of power over such large numbers of people and such large amounts of money. This attitude will change if the income from the Social Security tax is exceeded by the outlay; then the terms will be changed again.

Social Security is a Ponzi scheme, with changeable terms, under control of the

government. That makes it a <u>truly</u> high-risk investment.

Ponzi schemes are illegal. Except for the government, which is not subject to the laws that it lays down for the common folk. It may be advisable for individuals to put some 15.3 percent of their earnings into a retirement fund, but that should be an individual decision. The government has no reasonable excuse for running an "insurance" scheme that will soon be paying out at a negative interest rate.

CRIME AND PRICES

The public perception of common crime is shortsighted and constricted. This is because the true costs of crime are concealed and removed in space and time from any given incident. The careful consideration of a given criminal act will show the truth of this.

Suppose a robber holds up a convenience store and makes off with $125. What are the ramifications of this act in terms of cost? First, of course, the store has lost $125. But the store has installed a surveillance camera at a cost of $500, a cost made necessesary by possible/probable thefts. The wages of the clerk(s) must be somewhat higher to compensate for the possible danger of an attack, an ongoing cost. The store's business will be interrupted by the police investigation, and the public will be less likely to patronize a store that might expose them to risk. All of these costs must be made up by higher prices on the goods offered by the store, a cost paid by all customers of the store. Additionally, the cost of the police, investigation, capture and trial of the thief will cost a considerable amount of tax monies, a cost borne by all citizens. If the thief is incarcerated, the cost of the incarceration is added to the tax costs of the robbery and trial. All of these costs add up to 100 or more times the $125 of the original crime, but, in the public eye, the recognizable cost is the $125, not the hidden costs. This results in a public pressure against "unreasonable" punishments. Perhaps if punishment for crime was tied to true costs by some type of restitution, the costs to citizens in general would be lessened and the commission of crimes deterred.

Crime steals from us all.

If government is to be self sustaining (ideally) the cost of common crime should be made realistic, and the cost, as much as possible, should devolve upon the perpetrator *and those who enabled the perpetrator.* Currently, we make little or no effort in this direction. It is rare that any person convicted of a crime even pays back the immediate cost of the crime, and virtually never the extended social cost. Public apologies may be nice, but they do not replenish the public treasury for attendant outlays. The Constitution, in the thirteenth Amendment, contains a seldom-recognized provision that allows slavery as a punishment for crime. Perhaps we should consider it as a way of recovering the costs and discouraging petty crime.

WAR

War, it has been said, is politics by other means. This is the chief reason that there are so many wars. Politics is a popular game amongst a certain class of people who fancy themselves to be more suited than others to determine the fates of lesser persons. There is a certain low level of usefulness to politics and political games, as they provide a forum for large bodies of people to thresh out problems and differences without violence. This, of course, is a good thing, as violence often results in regrettable instances of otherwise blameless persons meeting their demise.

Most unfortunate, of course is when politics becomes mixed with religion, as it often does. There is no more powerful incentive to convince people to go to war than suggesting that their god or gods are being attacked and that their god or gods are approving and supportive of a war. The hijacking of religion has a long history, and assuredly goes back into prehistory. It is alive and well in the modern world amongst several Islamic nations. It should be noted that it is also widespread in a number of more secular nations when the god involved is Mammon.

Let us consider a touchstone here: if a war is

truly needed (and sometimes, indeed, only war will do), those calling for war should truly support it. In the past, kings often led their armies into battle, and even a few Popes have done so. George Washington led the rag-tag army of the new Republic into battle again and again, suffering with the troops in winter hardships and praying for God's blessings on their efforts. This custom is rare to non-existent these days, which, perhaps, speaks to the relative importance of today's wars.

When governments go to war, people die. Those people are seldom politicians.

The idea of placing those deciding on war into the fray where their lives would be at risk is certainly an idea worth considering. At the very least it would lend a certain gravitas to the decision to go to war, and at best it would convey to the citizenry at large that the war was truly important. It would also spur the search for effective alternatives to war. Imagine the end results if, in response to 9-11, President Bush had decided that an appropriate response to the actions of the terrorists and their homelands would be to eliminate their source of wealth, oil, by devoting the trillion-dollar cost of the Iraq war to finding a replacement for oil as an energy source, making the U.S. (and ultimately the world) independent of oil, thereby depriving the middle East of its source of wealth, and its ability to project harm on others. In the modern world, economic war may well be more effective and less deadly than the military kind. The following story may be instructive.

~~~~~~~~~~~~

THE WAR

(DON'T YOU WISH?)

THE PRESIDENT PATTED HIS STOMACH. "DAMMIT, THE FOOD IN THE WHITE HOUSE IS JUST TOO GOOD. LOOK AT THAT BELLY; I'M AS OUT OF SHAPE AS THE WORST COUCH POTATO, AND HERE I AM PRESIDENT. I SHOULD HAVE BEEN DOWN EXERCISING IN THE GYM."

THE AIDE NODDED. "YEAH, BUT YOU'VE GOT GOOD COMPANY. HALF OF CONGRESS LOOKS WORSE, ESPECIALLY SENATOR JACKSON."

"HEH! WELL, YOU'RE RIGHT ABOUT THAT. OF COURSE THE OLD FART IS NEARLY SEVENTY YEARS OLD. RECKON THAT HE'LL BE A GONER SOON." THE PRESIDENT TURNED TO OBSERVE HIS PROFILE IN THE MIRROR. "DAMN, I HATE THIS. WHY THE HELL DID I EVER GET INTO POLITICS ANY WAY? I COULD HAVE BEEN A POLICEMAN OR A DOGCATCHER."

THE AIDE SNICKERED. "THAT'S WHAT ALL POLITICIANS SAY, BUT THEY LIKE THE PERKS, AND THE PAY'S NOT BAD EITHER."

"SURE, BUT A MILLION A YEAR IS COLD COMFORT AT A TIME LIKE THIS. GOD, THE RESPONSIBILITY OF LEADING OUR ARMY, NAVY AND AIR FORCE INTO COMBAT IS A HUGE AND SERIOUS BURDEN. WHO'D HAVE THOUGHT THAT WE'D EVER GET INTO A WAR AGAIN? I MEAN AFTER A STRING OF DISASTERS LIKE VIET NAM, AFGHANISTAN AND IRAQ, YOU'D THINK THAT THE PUBLIC WOULD HATE THE IDEA. WE'RE STILL PAYING FOR IRAQ AND AFGHANISTAN, FOR PETE SAKES."

The aide nodded. "I suppose that the suicide bomber in Chicago had something to do with it," he observed dryly.

The President looked at the aide sharply, but the aide's poker face reflected none of the sarcasm that the remark implied. "Yes. A nuke for God's sake. How the hell could that get past us? I know, I know, a twenty-foot private sailboat coming up the coast, through the locks and across the lakes. And the assholes at Homeland were all looking at shipping containers. How the hell big do they think that a nuke has to be anyway?" He shook his head, and returned to examining himself in the mirror.

The aide nodded again. "Of course Afghanistan and Iraq are the main reasons for the War Amendment. That and Congressman Dent."

The President sat down and looked up miserably at the aide. "Yeah, Dent put that bill up to amend the Constitution because Congress had sloughed the war-making off onto the President, and thought that suggesting an amendment to make war subject to a popular vote would win him a few votes from the anti-war crowd. He was more surprised than anyone when it sailed right through the amendment process."

"With the rider from Senator Williams, of course," the aide reminded him.

The President nodded glumly. "Saying that all those drawing Government paychecks had to be in the front lines, in order of their salary." He adjusted the

LAPEL ON HIS UNIFORM. "HOW DO I LOOK?" HE ASKED.

THE AIDE SHRUGGED. "LIKE ANY PRIVATE FIRST CLASS" HE ANSWERED.

~~~~~~~~~~~~~

WHAT IS CIVILIZATION?

"Civilization" is an interesting, albeit a slippery idea. In order to have a civilization, there must be at least two people. One person, alone in a wilderness cannot be "civilized", for the very concept of civilization embodies the interaction between persons. Two or more persons may or may not be civilized. If two persons are alone in the wilderness, and they attempt to kill each other, we cannot say that they are civilized. On the other hand, if they cooperate with each other, we can say that they are acting in a "civilized" manner. The essence of this "civilized" behavior between our hypothetical pair in the wilderness is that they deal with each other on the basis of an agreement. The agreement may be as simple or as complex, as minimal or extensive as desired; it may be 'I'll stay out of your way, you stay out of mine', to 'you have my back, I have yours', or anything in between. The point here is that there is an *agreement*, a *contract*, between persons. This is the irreducible element in civilized behavior, and behind civilization itself.

Now any contract, in order to be a contract, involves three elements: volition, comprehension and mutuality. Volition means that each party to the contract must enter into it, or accept it freely; a person captured and subjugated into servitude is a slave – there is no contract, and thus slavery cannot be considered civilized behavior. On the other hand, a person entering into indentured servitude, indistinguishable on the surface from slavery, has made a contract of his or her own volition, wherefore this must be considered as civilized behavior.

The element of comprehension means that each party to the contract must understand the elements and conditions of the contract clearly. If one party lies or conceals portions of the contract, or if one party cannot comprehend the contract, no contract can exist. This is why most contracts are written. It is also why valid contracts generally cannot be made with persons of diminished intellect or between advanced civilizations and aboriginal tribes. (The purchase of Manhattan for some beads was probably not a valid contract).

Mutuality, of course, refers to the benefits and obligations between the parties. Each party must receive value and yield performance in return. To eliminate either value or performance on the part of either party denies the contract. Regardless of what the performance or value is, there is an inherent presumption that, since the parties have entered the contract voluntarily, the value to each party is equal to the performance from the other.

There is no inherent upper or lower limit on the contracts of civilized behavior. If one waits in a queue at a grocery checkout there is a contract, unspoken and unwritten: 'I will await my turn and, in return, you will too'. The person who barges into the front of the line violates this contract, and is acting in an uncivilized manner, regardless of how minor and ephemeral the contract may be. On the other hand, a fireman, agreeing to risk life and health to protect property and lives, in return for a wage, has made a contract of considerable gravity.

All this, of course, is why we distain the thief and the con artist – they make no honorable contract, thus act in an uncivilized manner when they steal or gull a victim.

When we honor our contracts, large and small, explicit and implicit, we act in a civilized manner and in doing so reinforce civilization. Breakdown of civilization begins when we ignore or disrespect our contracts, even the small implicit, contracts – the greeting not responded to, the trash littered, the wall tagged. We should act civilized, as it is to our advantage to do so, but it is easy to act uncivilized – our nature tends that way.

Civilization is not for sissies; it's hard, difficult work.

A wider recognition of the meaning and constraints of civilization should be a matter of basic education (there's that old education bit again). Probably a public equation of the keeping of all contracts, both written and implicit, with strength, honor and dignity, along with an equation of disrespecting such contracts with dishonor and weakness would go a long way, especially with youths, toward improving and strengthening civilization.

BUREAUCRACY

Virtually all governments produce bureaucracies in much the same manner that animals produce dung and, like dung, bureaucracy can increase in volume far beyond the actual government. The sole intrinsic purpose of any bureaucracy is to protect itself while increasing in size. This should not be doubted, as it occurs on a regular basis. One witness to this can be seen in the handling, by any bureaucracy, of leftover funds at the end of the fiscal year; there is an unseemly rush to spend every last cent, lest some money be "lost" by returning it to the system or, worse yet, to the taxpayers.

The ostensible purpose of any bureaucracy may be to enact certain public functions such as issuing and controlling vehicle licenses or overseeing public water works, but when one dissects the organization into its component individuals, little can be discerned other than a self-centered concern for their position, pay and benefits. Police, firefighters and military are the blatant exception, and in these, although bureaucracy certainly exists, it is minimal among those who are actually at risk, where the rubber meets the road, and it generally has a somewhat lesser hold on the rest of such organizations.

It would be well if there were a formal recognition of the nature of bureaucracies and procedures, beyond their reach, were in place to limit and regularly trim them. Recessions, competition and deflation serve this purpose in the market system, but there is no corresponding predator in the system of government. It would be a great benefit to the taxpayers at large if we could install a market type of competition in our governmental organizations.

A bureaucracy is a great mindless system run by dwarves.

A thought (or brain fart, as the case may be): would it be possible to set up opposing bureaucracies that are competitive and are paid on the basis of service? Would people (or politicians) freak out at the idea of the Seals bidding against the Green Berets? After all, we accept the idea of Boeing bidding against Martin or General Electric against Siemans for government contracts. Why not the efficiency of free enterprise within the government? "No, I don't pay that tax, it's a Democrat tax, I'm a Republican." Now there's a *real* brain fart!

BRIBING THE PEOPLE

Politicians make laws and create programs to entice money from contributors and to pander to their constituencies. Since neither the constituencies nor the contributors are inclusive of all or even a majority of the people, all laws and programs will discommode, offend, injure and just plain piss off large numbers and often majorities of the populace. This is one of the reasons that government employees, particularly politicians and administrators, are rated well below used car salesmen on the scales of trust and respect. This is not good.

People are bribed by politicians in a number of ways. Government funds for roads, a new government building in a certain state or district, a favorable tax deduction, etc. depressing etc. When these things are examined, they are tinsel and dross. Many of them are unneeded; airports in the boonies, bridges to nowhere and so on. Few are worth the price paid, the ultimate price generally being many thousands of times more valuable to the one who bribed the politician.

Politicians who brag about all the things that they have obtained for their constituents are really bragging about the bribes that they have taken, the favors they have done, and the extent to which they have depleted the public purse. These are acts of shame, not honor.

A politician who "brings home the bacon" has just given the rest of the pig to someone else.

Bribery is bribery, regardless of the terms that may be used to describe it. We should distain those who engage in it, not reelect them.

THE RESULTS

There is a certain mindset that values intent above results. Persons (and organizations) with this outlook assume that the most important consideration when solving a problem is the intent of those attempting the solution. The War of Poverty is a prime example of this concept moved into the political arena.

The War on Poverty was conceived as a means of lifting the poor of the country out of their mean condition and into a better life. In establishing the War, the politicians and legislatures made no scientific or statistical studies of the poor that they were attempting to help, nor did they look for examples of successful uplift programs. Hubris combined with ignorance and compassion to form the program pushed through Congress and into law. The results, as all the modern statistics bear witness, were an utter disaster. The welfare distributed placed the government in competition with young men who should have been husbands, expanding the illegitimacy rate, enticed young girls into single motherhood, underpinned poor work-free neighborhoods and devalued education. These results are with us today. The War created more of the poverty that it was intended to cure, mired millions in welfare that they could not escape since it paid more than entry level jobs and it left unattached men with free time to indulge in drugs and crime. The program was a trap for legislators as well, since it could not be repealed against the same emotional forces of hubris, compassion and ignorance that had brought it into existence and, worse, it produced its own self-interested entitlement-minded lobby and voting block.

Legislation, governmental (and some big business) programs are rife with this type of emotion-driven disregard of reality. Unfortunately reality has a way of dictating results that are quite divorced from intent.

It is very difficult for politicians, who are trying to please an emotion-driven electorate, to act on logic or to pay attention to empirical results. Things would probably be a lot better if they would.

By their fruits ye shall know them. (Jesus Christ)

Perhaps there should be an independent agency with the power to utterly destroy any government program, agency, law or legislation simply by fiat. Any such entity so destroyed would be *destroyed,* any employees fired, laws repealed, funding removed, fixtures and buildings sold, persons convicted released, works undone. Anything not set forth in the Constitution would be eligible. Its mission would be to consider intent versus outcome and act upon finding substantial discrepancies between the two. Think how much better off we would be, and how many trillions richer, if the War on Poverty had been killed after a couple of years' existence revealed its true fruits.

PETTY CRIME

There is a class of crime that we ignore. It is the type of crime that occupies the shadow-land between fully legal and the illegal, the window broken from an abandoned building, the tagged wall, the littered roadway, the junk filled vacant lot, the slow driver in the left lane or the battered mailbox. An entire class of such behavior lies in the verbal arena of angry language and impolite address. These types of wrongdoing may be malicious or thoughtless, but if thoughtless, the thoughtlessness has, in itself, an inherent maliciousness based on the conviction that others do not matter.

Petty acts such as these have two debilitating effects on the population at large. Firstly, there is the monetary cost. The windowpane will eventually need replacement, the wall will need to be painted, the litter will be picked up, the junk hauled away, the accident caused by the slow car, the mailbox that will need replacement. Individually these costs are small, some almost negligible, but in their totality they are substantial. The second effect is the most important: the message sent to the populace at large that criminal and impolite behavior, the impolite address is acceptable, that we have some sort of obligation to tolerate such.

Psychologists refer to such small acts as "gateway behavior" because of the effect that they have on both the actors and observers. Gateway behavior opens a conceptual pathway to more serious acts, the unstated conviction being that if small acts go unpunished or ignored, more serious acts will be as well. Cities that bear down on such petty crime find that overall more serious crime also declines.

It is sad that all too many think that attention paid to such small unsocial acts is silly, and should simply be ignored. They are wrong.

The true cost of social tolerance is concealed.

There should exist a category of crime one cut below the usual classification of "petty", with an independent enforcement system. In a rudimentary form this already exists in the form of the neighborhood scold who chides wayward children and complains about an unsightly lawn. The level of action (neighbor to neighbor) is right, but the formalization is missing. We once did this on an informal basis, but somewhere between suburbia and megopolis it has been lost, and we are the poorer and more endangered for the loss.

A program of sociological and psychological research might find ways of encouraging the reestablishment of such social intercourse. A careful vetting of researchers to establish that they have a pragmatic approach rather than the current fad for uberliberalism that currently holds sway in the social sciences would be necessesary for such research to produce real world results.

DIVERSITY

What the hell is "diversity"? Diversity is a buzzword that has taken over in all types of areas. The President wants diversity in his cabinet, without which he cannot govern properly, the schools are in desperate need of diversity in order for students to be able to learn, employers must have diversity in the workplace lest the wrath of the government be released upon them and fire fighters must be diverse, lest arsonists or whoever take umbrage. This is, of course, all a crock. There is no attempt to diversify on the basis of hair color, length of noses, political persuasion, eye color, vegetarianism, musical taste, snake ownership or ten thousand other possible vectors. The "diversity" so avidly sought by the politically correct addresses only "race" and "ethnicity", both of which are slippery concepts, which nobody has ever defined. This oversight is about to be corrected, so that we need no longer fight and argue over either term. Since such great store is placed on both "race" and "ethnicity", we will hereby define them, thereby clarifying the laws (if any) and rules (if stated) governing "diversity".

First, let us address "race". This term cannot be defined by means such as skin color, hair, nose shape, etc. since the range of these characteristics are smeared across all types, nationalities and classes of people. It would never do to classify Indians as "black" despite dark skin color, or Eskimos as "black" despite nose shape. We must turn to that irrefutable science of genetics to determine the meaning of this term. The politically correct "blacks" are those of African descent, more particularly, those from Western Sub-Sahara Africa. The DNA markers are distinctive. In order to receive the benefits of "diversity", a simple genetics test would suffice. In the interest of "fairness", we should establish a scale, since those whose DNA has been compromised by mixing with other genetic sources should logically not be entitled to as much "diversity" as those with more restricted backgrounds. A scale of 0 to 100 should suffice for most purposes. This would allow a neat mathematical method of assuring a proper amount of "diversity", wherever such is required.

Next, we must address ethnicity". Neither DNA nor physical characteristics can determine this, as it depends on the historical accident of the location of the various ancestors of the person in question and the changing borders of various nations in which those ancestors were located. For example, a person from Spain may have Arabic (from the Moors), Italian (from Spain's border), French (from assorted border incursions) and German (from mercenary soldiers) in their background. Here we must use a simplifying tactic, lest the formula become too complex for use and the climb up the familial tree becomes too exhausting. Let us arbitrarily set a limit of 2 generations back. If your maternal grandfather was German, your maternal grandmother Oriental, your paternal grandfather Russian and your paternal grandmother Oriental, you would be 1,Germanic, 1,Russo, 2,Oriental. If the particular organization in which you were involved needed Oriental diversity, they would be in luck, for you would bring 2 Oriental points out of 4 with you. If, contrariwise, they needed Eskimo diversity points, you would be useless to their achieving "diversity" of Eskimo points and you might be more warmly received in another organization.

I hope that this little exposition has placed "diversity" on a sound actuarial basis, so that we can all agree on what we are talking about. Henceforth we all should use these scales for expressing the amount and type of "diversity" which we have or need in any given organization.

Those who refer to ethnicity and race have an obligation to define their terms.

If anyone wishes to define himself or herself by race or ethnicity, they are separating themselves out from the rest of us as being somehow different. This is dangerous, for it makes them a target for prejudice and a resource for those who would exploit differences for personal profit or power. The world is better without such targets. This country has always drawn strength from being a melting pot, and it seems that the lumps in that pot tend to get stirred harder.

Ethnicity, race and diversity are pretty much un-American concepts. It may be simpler to simply forget about them.

NUKES

Shortly after WWII the public perception of the promise of nuclear energy was rosy. Life magazine and Time magazine both carried promises of electrical power too cheap to monitor – the connection to your home would not even have a meter, you would simply pay a small fixed fee and use all the power you wished. The promise was even fairly credible if somewhat exaggerated. The problem, of course, was that, as usual, the self- preservation instincts of business found willing allies in government and media. Horror stories of the dangers of nuclear power and radioactivity began to appear, climaxing in a movie starring Jane Fonda; 'The China Syndrome'. Seven years later the cherry was put on the top of nuclear/radioactive scare campaigns when the Chernobyl #4 reactor suffered a fire that spread radioactive contamination over a 70,000 square mile area. The Chernobyl disaster is credited with the death of at least 84,000 persons and possibly as many as 95,000. These are the only deaths that can be assigned directly to peaceful nuclear power, although the "peaceful" portion is open to debate, as Reactor #4 was designed (badly) to produce plutonium for nuclear weapons. The accident at Chernobyl sent the propaganda machines of oil and coal interests, along with their willing allies in the environmental movement, into overdrive, kicked off by a July 25th 1986 article in the New York Times by Serge Schmemann who tied a fanciful translation of the name 'Chernobyl' as 'wormwood' to the use of the term 'wormwood' in the Book of Revelations as a 'poison to the waters'. Government, driven by politicians sensing a useful crisis, jumped on the bandwagon, nearly legislating nuclear power out of existence in the United States.

Faced with the problem that nuclear power was relatively safe (balance the possible grand total 95,000 victims of Chernobyl against worldwide deaths of *1.5 million __per year__* resulting from the use of fossil fuels), some excuse had to be concocted to permanently smear nuclear energy. That excuse was the radioactive waste from power plants. The yearly air pollution from the average fossil fueled power plant amounts to over three million tons. The radioactive waste from a nuclear power plant for the same year is about one hundred fifteen pounds. The one hundred fifteen pounds is solid material that can be placed in a container. The three million tons is spewed into the air where we can filter it out with our lungs, drink it in our water, eat the mercury from it in our fish and trees can be treated by it to acid rain. The one hundred fifteen pounds, however, is *radioactive*, and will remain so for centuries. Somehow it has been postulated, it is impossible to get rid of any such waste. Actually this is true, because legislation, driven by political contributions from oil, coal and environmental interests, has blocked all reasonable safe ways to dispose of radioactive waste, leaving the waste to be stored on site at individual reactors. None of this could be accomplished without large donations to the pockets of politicians and their campaigns. The public has paid the price in death, environmental damage and treasure many times over. If nuclear power had continued on its original trajectory the 1997 goals of the Kyoto Treaty would have already been exceeded in the U.S. Each coal-fired plant replaced by a nuclear plant would have saved almost 130 lives per year, each oil-fired plant replaced would have saved 42 lives per year. These are significant numbers, but they are concealed from the ken of the public by time, distance and a lack of immediately observable causality. Nonetheless, our buildings and artworks are degraded, our forests are stunted, our children's lungs are blackened and our cancer rates edge ever upward.

Business has no business demanding

favors from government.

Business can gain advantages by bribing and otherwise helping politicians. It can do this because politicians are allowed to take contributions, as are their parties and campaigns. It can also do this because politicians can show governmental favoritism to selected businesses. Neither should be permitted. Considering that a portion of those 1.5 million deaths per year rests on the heads of the politicians and corporations that profited from oil, coal and environmental contributions, perhaps they should be hanging offenses.

UNIONS

In the early days of the industrial revolution, capital played an unduly powerful role. The wealth to fund equipment, buildings and machinery, by and large, came from the upper classes, which had already established wealth to draw upon. They also carried over the traditional distain for the lower classes. Labor was simply so many hands, available at the lowest possible price, to run the productive machinery. Being exploited in this manner tends to create unity amongst the exploited, however, with the result that groups began to form amongst labor to counter the power of capital. The result was a long series of often-bloody clashes, sabotage and other generally non-productive behavior on both sides.

The formation of unions by labor tended to balance the two sides of a productive equation. Machinery, financing, buildings and other capital investment were needed for production, as was labor to operate the production lines, transportation webs and all the other various aspects of the capital establishment. Additionally, labor is, by and large, the purchaser of the product of production lines. This balance was and is a precarious one, bounded on one side by the strike, on the other by the lockout. As with many conflicts in the civil arena, both sides have turned to government power, aligning roughly with the two political parties, using money and influence to produce favorable legislation. In this process, unions became simply businesses, supplying a product – labor. While unions were conscientious about their 'product', and endeavored to see that their workers were well trained and yielded good performance, the relationship between labor and capital did well. As with many human endeavors, however, unions became careless about quality, becoming simply collectors of dues and searchers for political influence, winning support from shortsighted members by upward pressure on wages and benefits without corresponding increases in skills or performance. As a result, unions became burdens upon some industries to the extent that those industries were destroyed or driven to other countries. These unions violated the first rule of a successful parasite: *do not kill your host.*

Unions should be one half of the productive equation, not a leech upon it.

A healthy union is a productive portion of the industrial equation. Labor without capital can produce virtually nothing and capital without labor is just so much stuff. This should not be an adversarial relationship; it should be a cooperative, joint effort, profitable to both sides. The introduction of government and purchased government influence into the relationship is destructive and unbalancing. It should not be permitted.

RESTRAINT OF TRADE

There is probably no more stabilizing force in the world than international trade, and there is probably no greater destabilizing force than the restraint of trade between countries. Trade stabilizes the relationship between countries because both parties see it as profitable, and it supplies goods that are desired or required by each. People do not like to lose money and, if the traded goods are necessities, the pressure to trade is virtually irresistible. On the other hand, if trade is blocked and money is lost or necessesary goods cannot be acquired, the pressure to turn to violence to replace trade cannot be quieted. A high percentage of the wars in the world have been fought over resources. It has been reasonably argued that Japan's entry into WWII was an outgrowth of Western restrictions on oil.

Trade is certainly the least expensive way to obtain almost any given resource, with the only obvious frequent exception being real estate. It is for this reason that the freedom to trade between people and nations is critical, and it should be a prime interest of governments to protect and increase trade. It is a sad fact of life, however, that many if not all governments consider the manipulation of trade to be not only a national prerogative, but also a desirable activity productive of tax income, influence and power. Additionally, the imposition of tariffs is often urged by internal citizens and companies, creating a fertile source of political clout. Those politicians and legislatures interfering with trade seldom appreciate that they are toying with war, or, if they do, may not care.

When trade does not cross borders, invaders will.

The fact that the Constitution allows government to arrange trade with other nations does not mean that it *must* do so. A great deal of trade between countries goes on without the government arranging anything, the subjects of this trade being beneath the immediate notice of the bureaucrats. This trade is often the fastest, easiest and most profitable and less subject to political manipulation. The only real justification (other than the opportunity for graft and political clout) for governmental interference in trade should lie in the area of military goods that could be turned against us. All else should be relegated to the free market.

FREEDOM

Nobody can look into the mind of a baby and discern genius, despite the fond imagings of all mothers and most fathers. Even as the child ages, there are no touchstones to indicate genius, and, indeed, genius is sometimes not recognized until long after death. It is no respecter of station in life, health or ancestry; it can reside in the stricken frame of a Hawking or a robust Leonardo da Vinci. Genius may tutor and grow under a fine educational system or in the absence of any formal system.

We do know one thing; freedom allows the greatest chance for development, whatever the type or brand of genius. What greater insights, what advances might have been made by Galileo if he had not been restricted by the Church? Would Einstein have flourished and been so productive if he had remained in Europe or would he have wound up in a concentration camp or the ovens? Would Islamic countries be as poor and restricted today if they did not discard half of their productive hands and minds by repressing women? In the miserable poor of Africa is there a lost mind that might have looked into the convoluted biochemistry of disease and found a cure for Aids or cancer?

Freedom is the tilled soil in which genius can

flourish.

The freedom to achieve, to become the best one can be, benefits not only the individual but, to an even greater extent, benefits society at large. Edison, Einstein, Tesla, Bessemer and hundreds of other innovators left us all immensely better off for their efforts, a legacy from which we all, from wealthy to poor, benefit.

The same freedom that nourishes the genius also permits and encourages the growth of more ordinary talent. No greater modern demonstration of this fact may be seen than in the present growth of India where, partially released from the bondage of a restrictive socialist system, individual achievement at a number of levels is flourishing. The lesson for all of us is clear – restrictions in freedom are paid for by a loss of individual development and achievement as well as a societal loss to all of us.

Freedom is important because it is the chance to be better.

The current governmental assault on our freedom robs us, as individuals, of more than our freedom – it also destroys our prosperity. It was for this reason that the Founding Fathers delineated the few things that a Federal government could do, and surrounded the citizens with lists of things that the government could *not* do. We have allowed this government to overstep its restrictions and do that which it should not do. A strict adherence to the Constitution would cure much of what ails the country. Some of the possible future dangers may be illustrated by this short, macabre tale.

~~~~~~~~~~~~~

THE FREE MAN

GUNTHER SORTED THROUGH THE HALF-DOZEN LOTTERY TICKETS IN HIS HAND, COMPARING THE NUMBERS WITH THOSE ON THE SCREEN. FINALLY HE SLUMPED BACK ON THE CRACKED UPHOLSTERY OF THE COUCH. "DAMN! ALMOST HAD ONE THERE — I WAS ONLY OFF BY TWO OF THE NUMBERS." HE LOOKED UP AT HIS VISITOR THEN SCANNED THE ROOM. "WHEN I WIN, I'M GOING TO GET NEW STUFF. BIG LAZY BOY AND A NEW RUG. HELL, I MIGHT EVEN GET A NEW PLACE, MAYBE A DOUBLE-WIDE." HE LAPSED INTO SILENCE.

HIS VISITOR NODDED. "WHAT DO YOU FIGURE YOUR CHANCES ARE OF WINNING?"

"AW, THEY GOTTA BE GETTING BETTER, I BUY TICKETS EVERY WEEK, SO SOONER OR LATER I'LL HIT IT. OL' JAKE OVER IN BLOOMINGWOOD ESTATES HIT FIVE GRAND A COUPLE YEARS AGO, AND HE ONLY BOUGHT ONE TICKET A WEEK." GUNTHER SCRATCHED AN ARMPIT REFLECTIVELY.

"YOU COULD BUY MORE TICKETS, OF COURSE. THAT WOULD INCREASE YOUR CHANCES."

"NAH, MY GOVERNMENT MINIMUM INCOME IS ONLY THREE HUNNER'T A WEEK. HEALTH DEPARTMENT SAYS I GOTTA SPEND NINETY ON FOOD THAT'S ON THE FOOD PYRAMID AND FIFTY ON HEALTH INSURANCE. HUD SAYS I GOTTA PAY THEM AT LEAST A HUNNER'T ON RENT OR MORTGAGE, AN' THE TAX ON THE MINIMUM IS EIGHTY. THAT MEANS I'M IN THE HOLE FROM TH' GIT-GO, SO I GOTTA FIND SOME WORK. THE BEST I KIN DO IS A BIT DOWN AT THE HIGHWAY DEPARTMENT THREE DAYS A WEEK, GETS ME TWELVE BUCKS AN HOUR, ABOUT EIGHTY A

WEEK AFTER TAXES. I DROP A FEW BUCKS DOWN AT THE CONVENIENCE STORE AN' GET A COUPLE TICKETS."

THE VISITOR NODDED. "LIFE'S TOUGH ALL OVER, I GUESS."

"DAMN RIGHT," GUNTHER AGREED, "BUT ELECTIONS ARE COMIN' UP. I'M SURE AS HELL GOING TO VOTE FOR FIELDMAN. HE'S GOING TO RAISE THE MINIMUM AND CREATE A LOTTERY DEPARTMENT TO MAKE SURE THE LOTTERY IS MORE FAIR. YOU HEARD ABOUT THAT GUY IN DELAWARE, WON THE LOTTERY THREE TIMES? THAT'S NOT FAIR. THE WINS NEED TO BE SPREAD AROUND MORE EVEN LIKE."

THE VISITOR SIGHED. "I SUPPOSE YOU'RE RIGHT. AT LEAST YOU'RE GOING TO VOTE. I SUPPOSE THAT MAKES YOU A FREE MAN."

GUNTHER LOOKED SUSPICIOUSLY AT THE VISITOR. "DAMN RIGHT I'M A FREE MAN. DON'T LET ANYONE BOSS ME AROUND. I'M AN AMERICAN!"

~~~~~~~~~~~~~~

THOSE AWFUL RICH

The "rich" are favorite scapegoats for all manner of politicians. In large part this is because politicians sense a source of ready cash through legislation designed to milk the wealthy. This has become so routine that some 90% of all United States income taxes are paid by the upper 10% of the income earners. The taxing of those who furnish nearly 80% of the nation's jobs, of course, tends to produce unemployment and to lower both GDP and thereby government income. This is one simple proof that the intent of politicians in taxing is not to raise revenue, but to raise votes through popularity and to amass power.

The persons who are so greatly productive that they rise into the stratosphere where they are so heavily taxed seem to regard the phenomenon with equanimity. This attitude is probably reinforced by a widespread notion that there is somehow a certain guilt attached to the attaining of such amounts of wealth, a public attitude aided and abetted by the aforementioned politicians. One sometimes wonders why they don't just retire somewhere, leaving the country in chaos, a la Atlas Shrugged. This attitude of the "rich" is most unfortunate for those who are of more common means, for, as mentioned, it is the wealth of these uberproducers that is largely responsible for the existence of productive companies and the vast majority of productive jobs in the country. If these "rich" were more perceptive of their actual function in society they would be more verbal and forthright in educating the country in regard their true function in the economic world. Nobody gets a job from a poor man or welfare recipient.

There is no Galt's Gulch. Fortunately.

The people want prosperity. The government wants money and power. These aims are in approximate conflict. The conflict is not total, because with prosperity comes more wealth. If governments could forgo power, they would find that greater prosperity and wealth could be had by minimal taxes on the rich, for it is they who create the jobs and businesses that elevate all, and removal of their money through taxes removes those jobs and, subsequently, the general wealth. The proper job of the government should be to simply keep us all honest.

PLANTATION POLITICS

There is a certain stripe of politician that finds political profit in separating groups by race and ethnicity. This is not new. A popular ditty during Roosevelt's rerun at the White House went; "You kiss the niggers, I'll kiss the Jews, we'll stay in the White House as long as we choose." Today's divisive politics are not as verbally blatant, but they differ in no other aspect. Today, the appeal is still separatist at its base, and has spread to include poor and excluded groups of all kinds. The appeal is that "we understand your isolation and feeling of powerlessness, and we will care for you." It is the political equivalent of the old plantations in the day of slavery; 'don't worry, just go along and you will be cared for, we know best.' That message echoes in multitudes of government programs, from welfare to social security, from health care to subsidized housing. These things are all fine if you wish to be a slave, but, as a people, we should have outgrown that by now.

Plantations, race and slavery are so yesterday. They should be ignored by all sides and left behind us.

Government should not concern itself with mothering the populace. There are a very few things that we need the government for, and wet nursing of select groups of people attracted to regressive, dependent behavior should not be one of them.

REALITY

There is a considerable disconnect between the "laws" written by man and the laws of the universe. The laws of the universe are impersonal, uniform and cannot be compromised or modified by feelings, passion, legislation, charity or any of the other human emotional failings.

It would be an admirable thing if human-made laws were to attempt to imitate natural laws in their immutability and evenness of enforcement. Mankind and, indeed, all creatures, have evolved in accord with natural laws, and these laws have shaped their existence. Unfortunately, human laws tend to be arbitrary, emotion-based and often inimical to health, prosperity and survival. Further, the enforcement of human laws is often excepted, ignored or imposed randomly.

Reality does not take account of poverty or wealth, goodness or badness, skin color or nationality nor any of the other arbitrary divisions that people invent to complicate their lives. There is a certain angelic purity in the operation of reality, a dispassionate consideration much lamented by emotionally driven persons who would prefer the world be shaped by their prejudices and controlled by their dispensation of rewards and punishments.

It is fortunate that a dispassionate God determined the rules by which reality operates, rather than leaving it to men.

In the real world there are no rewards, no punishments, only consequences.

Laws should be simple, direct and understandable. The Ten Commandments are an exemplary instance of good law; they are simple, direct, understandable by everyone and need no lawyers to interpret.

It would not be unreasonable to impose a limit of one side of one sheet of double-spaced twelve point Roman type for any given law. This would force lawmakers to actually think about their laws and omit the legalistic drivel that passes for lawyerly thought. There is a satirical article that circulates on the Net in which the Commandment "Thou shalt not steal" is rewritten in legalese. It occupies nearly 100 closely written pages. You can hide a lot of pork in 100 pages, even more in 1000.

There is great virtue in simplicity, and it is a virtue that should be intensively cultivated by those who write law.

WHY DO WE PAY TAXES?

Governments take money from their subjects, usually in the form of taxes. Since governments normally do not produce anything, they must garner money from productive sources in order to support themselves. Typically, this is done by taxation (ignoring, for the moment, such things as inflation, spoils of war, expropriation of property, etc.). The objects of taxation are almost infinitely varied; real property, income, gasoline, slaves, imports, exports, sales and, famously, tea have all been subject to taxation at one time or another and often many at the same time.

Now when governments get tax monies, they do a number of things with them. Firstly, of course, a certain portion is distributed amongst the members of the government. Secondly, some goes to defense, various social obligations and then the rest is divided in ways too numerous to mention –roads, bridges, airports, care of the poor, statues, arenas, law enforcement, fire and police protection, and so on, generally in manners intended to win political acclaim.

So why do we pay these taxes? Ask the question, and you will receive almost as many answers as people whom you ask. "It's the patriotic thing to do." " Someone must pay and maintain the army." "We have to have roads." "I suppose that you don't think that we need firemen and policemen." These answers may each have some validity, but they really don't answer the question: why do *you* pay taxes? Maybe you don't drive, so why pay taxes for roads? Maybe you are willing to risk a fire in your home or are willing to defend yourself for the sake of not having to pay taxes. So why do you pay taxes? Let me explain why by means of an example.

Suppose you are a tradesman, say a cobbler. You own a small shop (by own, I mean that you actually own it, bought and paid for). People drop in to have their shoes repaired, resoled polished, etc. You charge a fair price, you are satisfied with the payment; your customers are pleased with the service.

One day, a letter comes from the government asking that you remit twenty percent of your earnings to the government. Irritated at such presumptiveness, you drop the letter in the trash. Then a polite man comes from the government and demands that you pay the twenty percent plus a penalty for not remitting the money earlier. Irritated that anyone could presume to simply demand money from you, you kick that person off of your property as, being that it is _your_ property, you have the natural right to do. A bit later, a couple of not-so-polite men come from the government, insisting that you pay the twenty percent plus the now doubled penalty. You throw them, too, off of your property. Shortly thereafter another man will come from the government, and we must understand only one fact about that man:

He will have a gun.

And THAT is the reason you pay your taxes.

Behind all actions by the government stands the ultimate argument of brute force. That is the one thing that distinguishes governments and organized crime from ordinary entrepreneurial businesses. We do not like to consider this fact, and many people are in denial about it, but denial does not change reality. The presence of force is what _makes_ a government a government. If it were not present, people would pretty much ignore government, which would diminish it into usefulness. This is desirable.

SILENCE

Public speaking is an art and a talent. Some learn it and are passable speakers, but a few are naturals, talented talkers who grow more adept with time and practice. Now there are three main arenas in which a great speaker can prosper. The first of these is in salesmanship. A great huckster is worth his weight in gold to those seeking to sell anything from laundry soap and kitchen gadgets to cars. The second is the church, where a good preacher can enflame the spirit of the religious and inveigh the doubtful into the faith. The third is in politics.

The charismatic political speaker can sell the public on propositions of doubtful, perhaps even obviously non-existent, validity. Invariably the political hustler will appeal to prejudice, guilt, greed, sloth and most of the other seven deadly sins in his pitches. To those who operate on emotion rather than reason, the appeals of such persons are convincing and overwhelming, and the atmosphere about them is akin to a revival tent meeting.

In the milieu created by the charismatic politician, dissent and the voice of reason are not only absent, but actively suppressed, often with actual violence, but always with personal attacks. It takes a brave person to speak out against such political figures or their followers, but those who do so are our only warnings on the well-traveled road to perdition. This is one reason that freedom of the press (and media) is so important. Unfortunately, the media almost inevitably fall into thrall to such politicians, writing being akin to public speaking in concept and impact.

One person speaking makes more noise than 1000 who are silent.

The people who speak against propositions, laws and things in general - in short, the curmudgeons of society - are the persons who should be listened to. Their voices are hard to hear above the honeyed words of the smooth talker, but oftimes what they say has greater significance. The contrarian opinion, when expressed, at the very least engenders an examination of the facts. Speaking out on all matters political should be encouraged. There are times when silence is far from golden.

PROPHETS

Since time immemorial there have been prophets. Some preach oncoming doom (a perennial favorite), some prophecy the ascendancy of this or that group or nation while a fair proportion call down vengeance on those they consider unsanctified. Nostradamus made an enduring name for himself by prophesying in amorphous verses into which almost anything can be read. The practice, like Nostradamus, remains popular and widely employed to this day.

While religion is, and has always been, rife with prophets, many claiming behind-the-scenes support from God, a current and growing favorite is the political and economic prophet. The modern political or economic prophet generally frequents the airwaves, cable, Facebook and book stalls rather than deserts, soapboxes and village taverns as in days past. The extent of these various media has added the dimension of monetary return to the business of prophecy, and nowadays the prophet is most frequently dressed in suit and tie rather than sackcloth and ashes. The intent, however, is still the same - to convince as many as possible of the correctness of the prophet's idiosyncratic viewpoint.

The problem with political and economic prophets is that some few may be correct. They could just have a clearer insight into particular aspects of reality that have escaped the notice of ordinary folk and those that hearken to these persons may be benefited greatly. Those who called danger at Hitler's rise to power saved countless lives and those who saw market insanity in the twenties profited quite a few who attended to them. The problem thereby arises of how to distinguish those who are only talking to hear their heads rattle from those with true insight. One touchstone for such may be to observe whether the prophecies propounded directly produce wealth to the prophet, which is to say they are self-serving. A very large segment of political, investment and market advisers fall into this category.

Beware of the prophet who profits from prophecies.

We should all listen carefully to that which is propounded in the political or financial arena, and ask: "what will this person (or party) benefit from what is said?" If the answer is that little or no direct benefit to that person can be discerned, we can proceed to analyze the presentation on the basis of utility, safe in the presumption that we are not attending to a sophisticated panhandler or con man. We should also keep in mind that "benefit" may refer to that warm, fuzzy, elitist feeling that 'I know better than you what you need', so common amongst those who feel that their duty is to guide us.

MINORITIES

"Minorities" receive undue attention from the political elite. The reason for this is simple: a minority can be conned into both voting for and contributing financially to a politician. Both of these are dear to a politician's heart.

In order to be a useful minority for a politician, the minority must be somehow convinced that they suffer some sort of abuse or deficit, either real, imagined or potential, due to their being included in the minority designation. For example, the persons who were impacted by the hurricane Katrina have been easily convinced that the government has ignored them, and that the government has an obligation to succor them endlessly. In this can be found political power, largess and contributions. The number of minorities, thus determined, can be expanded almost without limit by propagandistic manipulation. Some, such as "women", are not even true minorities.

There are, of course, endless discernable minorities, such as redheads, bald people, short people, tall people, Catholics, Rotarians, people who live in trailers and skydivers. Most of these are not suitable for political purposes until someone can invent an abuse suffered by one or the other group. It also helps if there is some sort of outward manifestation of the minority membership, such as dark skin or living in a FEMA trailer.

The one truly tragic thing about the politics of minority pandering is that it submerges individuality into the politically more important group character, imputing thereby the deficits and abused state to all individuals in the group.

Minority politics detracts from and degrades the individual while only helping the politician.

The use by a politician of "minorities" as a political tool should be considered to be as inappropriate as a public bribe. The members of any "minority" so treated should be insulted. Being a willing political shill is hardly a noble civic undertaking, and any pittance of benefits that might accrue from such are surely outweighed by the shame and loss of dignity associated with same.

GERRYMANDERING

There is a tactic much abused by incumbent politicians of drawing electoral districts in such a manner as to insure that they contain constituents favorable to their reelection, or at least reelection of candidates of the ruling party. This abuse has led to electoral districts that meander along riverbanks, stretch tentacles from one side of town to the other through 100-foot wide corridors until they swell, amoeba-like, upon reaching a neighborhood of favorable voters. The result of constructing such districts is politics and therefore policies disconnected from both geography and population. Although putatively constructed to help certain minorities, such disconnects do not serve either individual voters, cities or counties well. They are only of service to politicians and political parties, and should not exist. They are often associated with pandering to minority constituents, with all the condescension that such fawning attention implies.

Gerrymandering is a tacit admission that the incumbent cannot command an honest majority vote.

There is a simple legislative tool to prevent gerrymandering; that is to make a statutory limit on the ratio between the length of the perimeter of a district and the area of the district. If the length of the perimeter in miles could not exceed the number of square miles enclosed by more than a 6:1 ratio, the abuse would be basically ended.

Eliminating gerrymandering, although it would probably eliminate a few edge clinging politicos, would bring a measure of honesty to elections that is currently missing. The practice is an unneeded remaining tatter of racial politics.

THE VOTERS

The attitude of politicians and legislatures toward voters is rather simplistic. They believe that the job of the voters is to elect them to office, and then to submit to the superior wisdom of the elite thus created. Somehow they assume that the voters must be sufficiently wise to determine that the persons to be elected are wiser than they, and that this wisdom is somehow limited only to such a determination and does not extend to any matters upon which said politicians and legislatures might act. It is thus that laws, programs and entire bureaucracies are often established despite the obvious objections of the electorate. It not infrequently occurs that not only legislators, but, indeed, presidents are elected on the basis of such smoke and mirrors.

On the whole, politicians believe that the people are too ignorant to know what is good for them and are incapable of ordering their own lives. They may be right – after all, we elected them.

It is the obligation of politicians and legislative bodies to listen to the people. They are allowed to act otherwise to our detriment.

Elections are intended to take care of

problems such as this. The fact that they do not do so is the fault of ignorance and sloth on the part of the voters as well as propaganda and ill reporting on the part of politicians and the media. The relationship between the media, politicians, legislatures and government in general is a poisonous one, the consumers of the poison being the public at large. The media should serve the voters, not the politicians or government.

LEAGALESE

Lawyers have a language all their own. It is convoluted, dense, difficult to understand and voluminous beyond all sense. The reason, of course, is that other lawyers will attempt to distort, misread and parse every word of any document with which they may have contention. We all laughed at Bill Clinton's "it depends on what the meaning of 'is' is" comment, but that was serious legal-speak. It is a sad thing that a such a high proportion of politicians are attorneys or have extensive legal training, for legalese is rampant in the bills and regulations put out by the government, assuring thereby endless secure employment for attorneys, judges and legal firms of all stripes. It is also a source of great expense for businesses and individuals who may be affected by these bills and regulations, wasting thereby immense amounts of time, treasure and manpower.

If a law or regulation cannot be read and understood by a person of average education and intelligence it has thereby failed in its basic purpose – to regulate the behavior of people in the arena addressed by the law or regulation, for how can it produce the desired regulation if it cannot be understood? This fact has been immortalized by the slang expression for a lawyer as a "mouthpiece", expressing the inability of common folk to effectively speak legalese.

So extensive has this type of creative writing become in our legislatures that even the legislators themselves admit to a complete failure to comprehend the bills upon which they vote, to the point that many do not even attempt to read them before voting upon them. This is a abdication of the basic obligations of legislators. So blasé have some of them become that they openly admit that they have voted without knowing that upon which they cast their ballot.

The U.S. Constitution, which governs (?) the country, occupies the equivalent of seven typewritten pages. Today's legislatures cannot write that brief a parking regulation.

Any law or regulation that cannot be clearly understood by at least ½ of a random sample of high school graduates should be considered void.

Clarity in our laws and regulations is of paramount importance to good lawmaking. Unnecessesary verbiage and convoluted definitions are only beneficial to attorneys. The laws should be addressed to citizens. Would it be unreasonable, in any jury trial, rather than a judge giving a simplified explanation of the applicable law to the jury (jury 'instruction'), that the jury would itself be constrained to read the law directly from the legislative acts? This might well lead to the demise of not only legalese but to the unemployment of great numbers of lawyers.

This would be desirable.

THE TECHNOLOGY TRAP

Government loves to control technology because with the control of technology comes the twin goals of government: money and power. This is not new; it is basic to governmental nature. When our nation was new, roads were made over trails, which had been made by men on foot following animal runs. When vehicles began to make twin ruts, defining the roads, government became involved, improving, defining and straightening the roads, which assuredly improved transportation and communication. With government, of course, came taxes on vehicles and fuel, for the roads had to be maintained. Bridges followed suit. Of course there are some private roads and private bridges, paid for by tolls, but they are minor and tend to be taken over by government. Then, too, with the need to build roads came the concept of eminent domain, a further extension of government power. Why didn't the roads and bridges become private enterprises? The same old two answers.

An example: as this is being written, there is an extensive movement afoot to make a central data bank with everyone's medical records. The concept is attractive on the surface, because a doctor or hospital can have all needed medical information on a person with a few keystrokes – invaluable in an emergency and very convenient in ordinary health care, tracking immunizations, etc. Of course this is to be a government program. The central data bank will employ a few tens of thousands of people and will cost a billion or ten to create plus many millions each year to maintain. But why? A simple, inexpensive system, which would cost the taxpayer nothing could be implemented by each person's medical record being transcribed into a memory chip, that memory chip to reside securely with each person as simply as a driver's license. Each person could be charged the dollar or two cost of the chip, the full medical record would be available to anyone the person wished, and could be easily updated at each medical visit or with each prescription filled. The only expense to doctors, pharmacists and hospitals would be the software, and the cost savings to them would probably be more than the expense of the system. The drawbacks to politicians are obvious – the government would not have a database to help control the health care of citizens and there would not be a corresponding expansion of governmental power and tax base.

Another suggestion that has been stillborn is entrusting the issuance of automobile licenses to insurance companies thereby tying proof of insurance to tag possession.

The instances in which government has corralled technological advances and turned them into government "services" subject to fees and taxes rather than allowing them to develop into private channels is almost endless, and each is an instance in which the citizen has been made more subject rather than more free. The next time you are dealing with a government service or entity, stop for a moment and ask yourself the questions: 'Could this be done by a private company? By individuals? Does it even need to be done at all?'

The power of technology should be used to increase freedom, not to diminish it.

Government should be "hands off" any new technology until it is fully deployed by industry and/or consumers. Once it is firmly in the public sector it should be safe to allow the government to have it, with the caveat that it could not subsequently regulate it, other than to prevent criminal abuses.

GLOBAL WARMING

Well, anyway it used to be global warming. Unfortunately for that title a string of several cooler years came along, and to keep from becoming either laughing stocks or from losing the public attention given to a fine scary, politically productive, scenario, 'global warming' was carefully morphed into 'climate change'. Climate change, of course, has an undeniably great advantage over global warming, since it can mean any variation from the status quo, whether that variation is heat, cold, more tornados, melting ice, unusual snowfall, etc. etc. This is almost foolproof, since the climate of the earth is in constant flux. There was a lengthy warm period from early 800 AD to about 1200 AD, with temperatures comparable to those of the last century. There then commenced a cooling period from 1200 AD to about 1700 AD which was so severe that the Thames river in England became a skating rink during the winter; in 1657 the Baltic froze over, and as late as 1780 New York harbor regularly froze over, allowing people to walk from Manhattan to Staten Island. We are, and have been for some time, in a warming period.

Now, historically, people have been better off during warming periods: crops are better, transportation is easier and energy use is less. During the cooling period noted above, glaciation increased to the point that entire villages were crushed and Greenland, heretofore a fertile land, as implied by its name, became icebound with floe ice as much as two miles offshore. In the geological past Antarctica has seen a temperate climate. The point, then, is that a warmer globe may be beneficial to humans. A few degrees overall consistent increase would almost double the earth's arable land, would open up the steppes of Russia to farming, allow grain crops to be grown well up into Canada, provide an ice-free Northwest Passage for ocean transport and let us grow oranges in Georgia.

You really have to hand it to the scaremongers who hope to stampede people into one or another political agenda. They have done such a thorough job of convincing everyone that any change is bad that a goodly portion of them believe it to be true themselves. It's not.

It is one thing to be scared of bad things, but making normal things sound scary is a propaganda masterpiece.

We should always be on the lookout for propaganda. If everyone suddenly believes something that has no observable reality we should examine the facts and make up our own minds, and the facts should not be those handed us by the suspected propagandist, particularly if the propagandist is a government or a politician.

Sometimes, a bit of private subversion may produce favorable results from a government program as shown in this fanciful short story.

~~~~~~~~~~~~~~~~

CLIMATE CHANGE

BENTO RAN HIS FINGERS OVER THE CHARTS, AS THOUGH HE WAS TRYING TO READ SOME ADDITIONAL INFORMATION INTO THEM THROUGH SOME SORT OF MENTAL BRAILLE. "LORD, NASA HAS BEEN TRACKING THE TEMPERATURE OF THE EARTH FOR FIVE DECADES. WE SHOULD BE WARMING UP WITH ALL OF THE CO_2 THAT PEOPLE HAVE BEEN PUTTING INTO THE ATMOSPHERE. WE'RE UP TO 860 PARTS PER BILLION, HOTHOUSE CONDITIONS; ACCORDING TO ALL THE COMPUTER MODELS THE TEMPERATURE AVERAGE SHOULD BE NEARLY THREE DEGREES CELSIUS HIGHER THAN AVERAGE. INSTEAD, WE'RE GETTING COOLER. IT'S DOWN AN AVERAGE OF $1/2$ DEGREE CELSIUS OVER THE PAST DECADE. THE POLITICOS ARE CRAWLING ALL OVER OUR BACK. THE WORLD'S GOVERNMENTS HAVE SPENT TENS OF TRILLIONS TO CAP GREENHOUSE GASSES. IF THEY HADN'T THE CO_2 WOULD BE OVER A THOUSAND BY NOW. THE CO_2 GOES UP, BUT TEMPERATURES GO DOWN. IT LOOKS LIKE ALL THAT MONEY HAS GONE TO WASTE."

GRAMMERSON SHRUGGED, AND ROLLED UP THE CHART. "ACTUALLY IT'S A HUNDRED TRILLIONS IF YOU COUNT THE EUROPEAN PUSH AND THE CHINESE INITIATIVE" HE SAID. "OF COURSE ALL THE PLANTS LOVE IT. ALL THAT CO_2 HAS SPEEDED UP PLANT GROWTH 10 TO 15 PERCENT. LOT LESS HUNGER IN THE WORLD NOW. BIGGER CROPS, RICE ESPECIALLY."

BENTO NODDED. "YEAH, THERE'S THAT, BUT ALL THE MODELS SAY THAT IT SHOULD BE GETTING WARMER, NOT STAYING THE SAME OR MAYBE GETTING COOLER. AFTER ALL, WE'RE SUPPOSED TO

BE COMBATING GLOBAL WARMING, NOT TRYING TO IMPROVE CROP YIELDS. WORSE YET, THEY'RE TALKING ABOUT DEFUNDING NASA. TALK ABOUT KILLING THE MESSENGER!"

"UNH HUH", GRAMMERSON ACKNOWLEDGED, "BUT A LOT OF THOSE MODELS ARE OURS. WE'RE NOT JUST THE MESSENGER, WE'RE RIGHT THERE IN THE GOVERNMENT'S POCKET, PREDICTING A RISE OF FOUR DEGREES AND SEA LEVEL INCREASES OF THREE OR FOUR FEET WITH THIS MUCH CO_2. SO SEA LEVELS HAVE DROPPED ONE INCH IN THE LAST TEN YEARS. DOESN'T LOOK GOOD FOR US, HMM?"

BENTO NODDED. "WELL, THEY CAN HARDLY DEFUND US COMPLETELY. THE MOON COLONY IS COMING ALONG FINE, AND THEY STILL NEED SUPPLIES, NEW PERSONNEL, AND SUCH. THE HEAVY HYDROGEN THEY'RE REFINING FROM THE REGOLITH HAS BECOME A COMMERCIAL SUCCESS, AND WE WOULD BE IN A WORLD OF HURT IF THAT WERE TO BE CUT OFF. WHAT DO YOU MAKE OF THIS" HE UNROLLED THE CHART AGAIN AND TRACED A LINE ON IT FOR GRAMMERSON, "UV RADIATION AT THE SURFACE IS UP ONE AND A HALF PERCENT. NOT MUCH, BUT THE OZONE LEVEL HAS THINNED SOMEWHAT, THE ADDITIONAL CO_2 PROVIDES SOME EXTRA SHIELDING. ODD, ISN'T IT? YOU'D EXPECT THE EXTRA CO_2 TO DROP THE UV LEVEL."

GRAMMERSON SHRUGGED AGAIN. "ALL WITHIN THE ERROR PARAMETERS," HE ASSURED. "PEOPLE WILL JUST TAN ONE MINUTE FASTER, CROPS WILL GROW A BIT FASTER, SUNGLASS SALES WILL INCREASE. BIG WHOOP."

BENTO SMILED. "YOU'RE RIGHT, NOT ANYTHING TO WORRY ABOUT, FAR TOO SMALL A

CONCERN NEXT TO THIS GLOBAL COOLING. SHIFT GEARS A MOMENT. HAS GENERAL HYPERBOLIC DELIVERED ON THE NEW ROCKET FUEL FOR THE MOON SHUTTLE? LAST I HEARD THERE WAS A DELAY. WE CAN'T AFFORD TO DROP BELOW A ONE MONTH SUPPLY ON HAND, WITH THE MOON SHUTTLES GOING UP ONCE A WEEK."

GRAMMERSON SHOOK HIS HEAD. "JUST A SEASONAL ADJUSTMENT. THE FORMULA VARIES A SLIGHT AMOUNT ACCORDING TO TEMPERATURES AT THE LAUNCH SITE. IT ASSURES MAXIMUM EFFICIENCY. THE COOLER WINTER TEMPERATURES MEAN A BIT OF A DIFFERENT FORMULA BALANCE. NOT TO WORRY, I HAVE GOOD PEOPLE ON IT, AND WE WON'T LET IT GET AWAY FROM US. IT'S JUST," HE SMILED MISCHIEVOUSLY, "GLOBAL COOLING."

BENTO SNICKERED. "GOD, I'M GLAD TO HAVE A GENERAL MANAGER LIKE YOU. YOU ALWAYS KEEP ON TOP OF THINGS AND MANAGE TO KEEP YOUR SENSE OF HUMOR. THIS GLOBAL COOLING JUST MEANS THAT WE SHOULD GET OUT OF THE PREDICTING BUSINESS, RUN A BUS SERVICE TO THE MOON AND BACK, GO EXPLORE THE PLANETS. LEAVE GLOBAL WARMING OR COOLING TO THE POLITICIANS TO ARGUE OVER. WISH WE HAD SOME OF THOSE TRILLIONS OF DOLLARS THEY'VE SPENT ON THIS, THOUGH."

GRAMMERSON NODDED AND REROLLED THE CHART. "I'LL GET ON GENERAL HYPERBOLIC RIGHT AWAY, CHECK ON THEIR DELIVERIES. YOU'RE RIGHT, WE NEED THAT BUFFER OF A FEW WEEK'S FUEL."

***

GRAMMERSON, BACK IN HIS OWN OFFICE,

TURNED ON THE SECURITY SYSTEM, PICKED UP THE SECURE PHONE, PUNCHED A NUMBER IN. "GENERAL HYPERBOLIC," A PLEASANT FEMALE VOICE ANSWERED, "HOW ARE YOU DOING SWEETIE?"

GRAMMERSON RELAXED. "DOING GREAT, MARY. LOOK, ON THIS NEXT DELIVERY OF FUEL FOR THE SHUTTLE, YOU NEED TO DROP THE SULFUR DIOXIDE BY A COUPLE OF POUNDS PER MILLION. THE STUFF IS WORKING TOO WELL, WE'RE ACTUALLY ON A GLOBAL COOLING CYCLE. WE'RE PUTTING TOO MUCH SUNSHADE IN THE STRATOSPHERE, THE SHUTTLE'S EXHAUST HAS GLOBAL TEMPS DOWN HALF A DEGREE THE PAST DECADE."

"O.K." MARY REPLIED. "WE'LL JUGGLE THE FORMULA A BIT. ANYTHING TO SAVE THE PLANET," SHE GIGGLED. "IT'S SURE EXPENSIVE THOUGH. YOUR LAST CHECK BARELY COVERED THE COST."

"IT'S A PERSONAL CHECK, MARY. YOU COULD ALWAYS KICK IN A BIT, YOU KNOW. DON'T WORRY, I CAN AFFORD THE SIXTY FIVE DOLLARS A WEEK FOR A FEW POUNDS OF SULFUR."

~~~~~~~~~~~~~~~~

RIGHTS THAT AREN'T

The U.S. Declaration of Independence points out a salient fact: that governments draw their "just powers" from the people. The principle at work here is that all rights inhere in the people, and that the people delegate certain of those rights to the government so that those rights may be more effectively exercised. For example, all persons have the right to defend themselves against those who would harm them. In order to effectively exercise those rights, they delegate their government to defend them by means of police, judges and armies. By this means the right to defense of a number of citizens is grouped together and made more effective than if the citizens only exercised it individually. A thief does not have a right to steal from others, so the "right" to steal from people cannot be delegated to the government. It should also be pointed out that the government does not 'permit' citizens to have rights, nor does it 'grant' citizens rights. The reverse is true.

To understand the legitimacy of government actions in terms of the rights delegated to it, we must first consider the nature of rights. Rights can, obviously, only inhere in individuals. There are no free-floating rights lying about waiting to be picked up. The very concept of a right defines it, for no person may posses a "right" that injures the right of another. By their nature rights cannot be in conflict. For example there cannot be a "right" of one person to injure another, for such a right would conflict with the other individual's right to life and liberty. This being the case, a governmental action that infringes upon an inherent right of an individual is, by nature, unjust, there being no way that the government could obtain such a right from its citizens. All governmental agencies and actions should be judged with this principle in mind. No citizen can have a "right" to housing, food or medical care, for to have such a "right" others would be forced to supply these things, thereby damaging their rights.

The legitimacy of government arises from the delegation of citizen's rights. Citizens cannot delegate non-existent rights, nor should government pretend that they can.

The government, to reapply Benjamin Franklin's words, "should neither a borrower nor a lender be". It should accept the delegation of the citizen's rights as a sacred trust, and should keep them intact, neither adding to them nor subtracting from them.

MONOPOLIES

Capitalism is a very effective means of maximizing efficiency in the production, sales and distribution of goods. It does suffer from one illness, however, which it shares with government-- - the propensity to generate monopolies. Just as with government, which is a natural monopoly, a business that becomes a monopoly loses the efficiency, innovative edge and drive for improvement that results from competition, becoming thereby stagnant and moribund. The Federal government has, from time to time, broken up monopolies that have impinged upon what was perceived to be the public interest. There is no apparent mechanism in the capitalistic system to prevent monopolies – indeed, it is the natural tendency of any business to become a monopoly and dominate its sector of the economy and the intervention of the government probably has been beneficial.

Unfortunately there are no hard and fast guidelines to determine that a business has become a monopoly in need of being broken up. Certain things are natural monopolies, such as the delivery of electricity and other physical utilities, there being no economic way in which competing services could be furnished. This is the drive behind government regulation of utilities, preventing them from price gouging. (Note that in the case of utilities it is the *delivery* system that is the monopoly. Any number of companies could furnish electricity, water, sewage service, etc using the same delivery system.) It is well to also point out that some apparently natural monopolies may be broken by technology, much the way broadcast TV was by cable, satellite, optical line and the computer.

We can see from the above that there are actually two types of commercial monopoly, one that comes from a business that grows to encompass either most or all of its field, and another, like the delivery systems for utilities, that occurs because of the expense of needless duplication. The heavy hand of government in the form of regulation and the equally heavy hand of oversized business monopolies are a drag on freedom and the economy.

Government is, by nature, a monopoly. Corporate imitation of government does not improve the situation.

The restriction of monopolies could be reasonably relegated to the courts, as could regulation of natural monopolies. Perhaps a mandate that past a certain size corporations, amoeba-like, would divide into two or more entities would be beneficial.

Allowing government to regulate the breakup of monopolies tends to be capricious, random and subject to corruption. The intent of breaking up a monopoly is to engender a healthy competition. All too often government breakups result in incestuous relations between companies and a far too intimate relationship with the government.

ECONOMIC BIRTH CONTROL

If you are one of the bold sort who desires to take your destiny in your own hands and begin your own business, you will find that there are many problems you must face and many difficulties that you must overcome. Many of these are intrinsic to the nature of your particular undertaking. If it is a restaurant that you wish to open, you must find a good location, a building, equipment, cooks, waitresses, etc, etc. Most of these things are obvious, and can be anticipated and planned for. Equally, however, there are governmental hurdles to jump, problems placed in the way of the entrepreneur that are not intrinsic to the business. These include permits, business licenses, inspections, tax forms, special bank accounts for withholding taxes, IRS registration, sales reporting, property evaluations, inventory reports, etc, etc. Generally these governmental requirements are aimed at providing the a basis for various taxations, permit fees and control over the business. This can extend to refusal to issue permits if the powers that be determine that a particular business should not be located in a particular area, that it would be too competitive with already existing businesses in the area or that it might upset the tender sensibilities of nearby neighbors.

The control of governmental bodies over the various aspects of business acts as a deterrent to the creation of new enterprises and the jobs that such might create. It is a form of birth control on new undertakings, and much of the licensure and taxes are instigated by already existing businesses' pressure on politicians to limit competition. If business is taxed, the price increase is passed on to its customers, and this is simple enough, but the deliberate creation of barriers to business creation and operation are a non-productive tax that detracts from general prosperity.

Government should not take sides in the marketplace.

The marketplace has many natural forces that tend toward efficiency, benefiting us all. Indeed, it is this drive toward efficiency that makes the free marketplace so effective an instrument for generating wealth and jobs. Government intrusion benefits nobody in the long run, and in the short run discourages innovation.

Few will dispute that simple requirements such as safety, building standards and such are beneficial, but such oddities as "occupational licenses" and "business permits" are nothing but taxing measures. Best be honest about it and create a single, simple tax requirement. The saving in accounting expenses and manpower would be worthwhile for all concerned.

US SOURCING

People talk a great deal nowadays about 'outsourcing' and 'insourcing' – the processes of moving work to where the labor, facilities and/or expertise are most profitable. We outsource our order processing, computer troubleshooting, product support and ordering to India, our toy and gadget manufacturing to China, our machine tool manufacturing to Japan. We insource customer contact, from salesmen and representatives to websites and online help. This is all done in pursuit of efficiency, lower cost and better quality.

Governments do not do much insourcing or outsourcing for very good reason. In order to do either, you give up a certain amount of money, a certain amount of control. Both are anathema to a government. Here's a thought, however. Why not us source?

What is us sourcing? Turning back some of the functions of government to the control of citizens and companies – to us. I don't mean simply hiring outside firms to do work for and to be paid by the government, a la Blackwater, but the government actually shedding the functions and relegating them to the individual citizen or company. For example: why does the government issue marriage licenses? What concern is it of the government's to identify the connubial state of private citizens? If some wish to be married in a religious ceremony, fine, that should be their business. Why should the government extend special privileges (and special taxes) to married vs. unmarried citizens? On a different note, why does the government make and maintain roadways? The few private or semi-private toll ways are usually far superior to regular roads. Why shouldn't roadways be commercial private ventures? If private companies ran roads, collected tolls (presumably by automated electronic means), they would have every incentive to make them more efficient and to maintain them well in order to keep and increase ridership, while eliminating the need for license plates and fuel taxes. In all probability, of course, if we explore the possible return of governmental functions to the citizens we will doubtless find a large number of things, for which we now pay tax monies that just don't need doing at all.

Freedom is not measured by what government does for us, but by what we do for ourselves.

Allowing or demanding the government to do for us that which individuals or the private sector is able and willing to do should be forbidden, for each thing done for us by the government is a freedom lost. If a private source offers to perform a function that is done by the government, and shows the ability and willingness to do so at an equal or lesser price and equal or greater quality, it should be mandatory for the government to relinquish that function to the private sector.

MAKING CHOICES

The practice of democracy through the vote is a process of making choices. The United States is a great experiment in allowing the people to vote for their leaders, even if indirectly, thereby choosing those who would govern them. In order to effectuate a republican democratic system it is necessesary that the people have liberty, for the coerced vote is not a vote at all, Mr. Castro's protests notwithstanding.

Unfortunately there is no guarantee that the vote will be used wisely or with intelligence. For this, it is necessesary to have an educated populace; a badly educated and propagandized populace is in a poor position to make wise choices. It is for this reason, that certain groups recognize education as the Achilles heel of the American republic. The vote is one of our most precious civic possessions, and our liberty lies in the right to choose. Freedom is the result of our making the right choices.

Guarding our educational system from corruption of standards and from those desirous of inserting their political beliefs into the education of our youth should be a primary concern of all, so that our citizens can make an educated choice. Simply voting does not ensure a desirable outcome; the vote must be informed and thoughtful.

The question, then: is it wise to place educational responsibility in the hands of government, to be paid for with monies collected and controlled by politicians?

Education should be private, individual – and a prerequisite to voting.

Poll taxes are illegal, and for good reason – even a well-educated and wise voter can be impoverished. Education, however, is another matter. We remove the franchise from mental patients and criminals, which is eminently reasonable, for it is not sensible to allow the criminal and the deluded to guide the ship of state. Education in the matters upon which one is voting is only sensible and prudent, but enactment of a measure to require a minimal knowledge of the subject(s) is fraught with problems. In the wrong hands (of which there always seems to be a plentitude) this could be more regressive than a poll tax.

It might be cumbersome, but perhaps each ballot could be prefaced by a short video made by the proponents (or candidate) setting forth the intent of the legislation or the platform of the candidate, although keeping *that* free of propaganda would be problematical. However accomplished, assuring that the voters have at least a minimum amount of information about what they are voting on should have a high priority.

GOVERNMENTAL NECESSITY

There are a few things government does for which nobody has ever found an adequate substitute. This is not to say that no substitute is possible; only that none has been found or designed. Predominant amongst these are the common defense, the creation and maintenance of a medium of exchange, uniform enforcement of laws and regulation of the commons. As with most things governmental, our government does a rather poor job of all four. Let us examine these four in brief.

Common defense refers, of course, to the military and the protection of the nation and it's citizens. By and large, the country is well defended, although there is considerable lack of agreement as to whether or not foreign adventures, military stationed abroad and the unrewarded defense of our neighbors should be considered 'common defense'. The military is expensive, perhaps needlessly so. There is some value to the argument that being a good friend and a fearsome enemy requires much less expensive military brawn, engenders less envy and hatred, and is a more effective defense.

One of the stickiest wickets concerning governmental function and responsibility is the common defense. We can hardly rely on a private armed force, since the concentration of force in the hands of a few has traditionally led to abuses by governments and the creation of dictatorships. A national army, supported by taxes, drawn from the population and answering to the population at large has proven itself a viable solution to possible abuses. If the source of the military personnel is the population at large, it will generally be well regarded by the people. The monetary support of the military is the crux of the problem. In order to be fair, all citizens who are protected by the military should share in the expense. Since there is no presumed difference between the value of individuals, the share of expenses should be equal for all. The problem, of course, is that the individual share of expense could be so high that it would impoverish a number of low-income persons. Rather than going to a "progressive" solution, a provision to allow anyone so desirous, to substitute time and effort in place of money or in addition to money could be included along with the general tax provision. Even persons of some means might be inclined to donate time and skill rather than simply money, especially as such would most likely be seen as honorable and patriotic, and could well be a plus on a civic or political resume. There is also the reasonable possibility of universal (meaning *everyone*) conscription. This has the added advantage that all citizens would be trained in the use of arms, creating an enormous reserve of armed forces in the event of hostilities.

The defense of the commons – air, water, wilderness, fish, etc. has an extremely poor record with virtually all governments, as environmentalists are loudly and tiresomely informing us. Most thinking people will readily agree that government just isn't up to the job of protecting our commons, or, at least, hasn't shown great capability in this area to date.

Now, there are certain things that, by their nature, are shared in common by either all or by large numbers of persons but are owned by none. The most obvious of these are air, moving surface water such as rivers, large lakes, the oceans, fish, wild animals at large and aquifers. The problem with these arises when the question of value to the individual is considered. If the article in question is of intrinsic value, such as whales, or has value in being used, the more acquired or used by the individual, the more that individual benefits. For example, a river may be used for sewage disposal by a few, destroying the value of the river as a source of potable water for many. The simplest way to handle this problem is by removing the article from the status of a commons and make it private property. If, in the example above, the river was owned (presumably by a corporation or other organization), that owner would conserve and care for the property, allocating the usage in the most profitable manner, and thus in the most useful way. The owners would scarcely allow the river to be polluted by sewage, destroying its value as salable drinking water and a profitable recreation source. There are, naturally, some resources that cannot be so managed, such as air or oceans, but these could be sensibly handled by legal means and determinations of responsibility, for example, an atmospheric polluter being responsible for damaging those affected by the pollution. This is already established in current law, but could be beneficially extended and refined.

All civilizations require a medium of exchange, whether gold, dollars, euros or wampum. The existence of a medium of exchange implicitly includes a means of regulating it, producing the physical and/or virtual coinage and a means of protecting it against adulteration through forgery. Having the government in charge of the medium of exchange has, historically, proven to be treacherous. The government of the U.S. in the last century absconded with virtually all of the gold in the country, eventually yielding unsecured notes in return. Government always wants more money than it has, and the temptation to monetize a debt by printing money has proven irresistible to many, if not a majority, of governments. It certainly has for our current government – the dollar has been inflated by additional printed currency by about 2500% to date. This is why earlier monetary systems were based on gold, silver or other difficult to obtain materials. Even this system, though, was abused by deliberate adulteration. Further, gold and silver based currency suffered from deflation in prosperous times as goods or services outstripped the money supply or any possible increase in the rate of circulation. This is, however not a bad thing – it makes saving very rewarding. Our government allows a slow but definite rate of inflation, which cheapens our currency, a practice followed by most modern nations. This steadily reduces national debt and robs the citizens with a hidden tax, which disproportionately impacts savings. The rate has been increasing rapidly in the last couple of years.

Money, although not necessesarily the root of all evil, is certainly the source of much evil, especially governmental evil. Allowing a government to create fiat money is to place children to guard the cookie jar. A commodity based monetary system has the potential for ultimate stability, wherein a dollar will always be valued the same regardless of time. Gold and silver based systems are historically the best, however the fact that silver and gold have become of commercial value in medicine, electronics and other applications interferes with their viability as bases for a monetary system. The advent of the computer and the ability to collect, manipulate and evaluate huge amounts of information has opened a new possibility that is worth considering. A monetary system based upon the total value of the country, all of its products and assets, continually updated, would provide a basis for a monetary system that could not be easily corrupted. It would, further, encourage a government to avoid any action that would decrease the assets or the value of the assets of the country and would encourage actions that would increase them. The main problem would be to assure the honesty of the data collection. Probably dispersing this responsibility to owners and producers would produce some assurance against corruption. This would be the ultimate commodity based monetary system.

The very basis of civilization depends on law and the acceptance by the population of that law. Key to that enforcement is the perception of the citizenry at large that those laws are enforced fairly and uniformly. In its early days, the United States government did an excellent job of this, and that contributed greatly to our growth, giving a stable and predictable environment in which business could grow and flourish. Governments being governments, this has deteriorated to the point that today two-thirds to three quarters, (some estimate as high as 90%) of all government activity is done in defiance of the Constitution, presumably the guiding law for what the government may and may not do. Laws are regularly bent, amended and made flexible to our detriment.

Is it possible that a private means could be found, developed or invented to handle these areas of government? A means of common defense not in the hands of the government and yet not a threat to others or ourselves? A system of currency that is completely stable so that there is no inflation or deflation? Some means to protect our valuable commons so that they are not diminished or over-exploited? We should not dismiss these possibilities out of hand. It was once considered absolutely neccessary to have a government postal system – so much so that it was enshrined in the Constitution. They just didn't have e-mail, UPS or Fed-Ex and when these came along, the Post Office became moribund.

Possible private solutions to government functions are neither researched nor even considered as worthwhile areas of investigation, and yet they lie at the heart of our civilization.

We only need government because of a few things. We should strive to reduce, not increase those things.

The steady reduction of governmental responsibilities and the corresponding concentration of government effort on the remaining responsibilities would result in a freer country and a more prosperous and powerful economy. It would also reduce the size of government, increasing thereby the money and effort available to improve the general welfare. These are all good things.

ON VOTING

How often, when voting, have you been undecided, feeling that the choices put forth are between poor and poorer? Laws, constitutional amendments, taxes, politicians and general civil matters are often put to the vote, and the results are hailed as inspired and widely (depending on the vote margin) desired, when the reality is that the populace at large was simply voting on what they consider the lesser of two evils. All this, of course is one of the basic reasons that so many of our laws do not function the way that people expect. When laws are designed, they, like the making of sausage, cannot easily bear scrutiny in regard to content. Since politicians acknowledge themselves as experts in almost any given field, there is generally little input from those with real and practical knowledge in the field being legislated upon. (This shows, as when, in a recent law intended to ban polyethylene bags, the law was drafted to ban polypropylene bags.) The result is laws that are off target, often detrimental, and sometimes antithical to the original intent of the framers, and yet people, including politicians, hold their noses and vote, being somehow under the impression that the vote is *needed.*

Wouldn't it be nice if all votes, both in

legislatures and elections included the choice: 'none of the above', a mandate to return to go and start over again if it received a plurality?

When you choose between two evils, remember – your choice is still evil. (Max Lerner)

The idea of including "none of the above" in all ballots (and, hopefully, all legislative votes as well) has been bandied about for a long time. It is an idea whose time has come, despite the wails of politicians everywhere. Their discontent with the idea is a direct indicator of the concept's desirability.

~~~~~~~~~~~

THE GENIE

THE UPCOMING ELECTION, GENE KNEW, WOULD REALLY BE A SQUEAKER. THE POLLS GAVE HIM A RATING OF 42% TO HIS OPPONENT'S 43%. IT WAS SCARCE COMFORT THAT THE DIFFERENCE WAS 'WITHIN THE LIMITS OF UNCERTAINTY' FOR THE POLL. AFTER LONG AND HESITANT CONTEMPLATION, HE DECIDED THAT THE TIME HAD COME TO OPEN HIS FATHER'S CHEST. NOW, IT SHOULD BE UNDERSTOOD THAT GENE'S FATHER HAD BEEN A FAMOUS AND SUCCESSFUL STAGE MAGICIAN, AND IN HIS WILL HE HAD LEFT A SMALL CHEST TO GENE, WITH THE STRICT INSTRUCTION THAT THE CHEST WAS TO BE OPENED ONLY WHEN GENE WOULD FIND HIMSELF IN TRULY DESPERATE STRAIGHTS. THE CHANCE THAT HE WOULD NOT BE REELECTED AFTER A LIFETIME IN THE SENATE WAS, HE FIGURED, TRULY A DESPERATE STRAIGHT, SO, AFTER A TIRING DAY OF STUMPING, HE RETIRED TO HIS COMFORTABLE TOWNHOUSE (PURCHASED FROM A GRATEFUL BUSINESSMAN FOR 25 CENTS ON THE DOLLAR) AND TOOK OUT THE CHEST.

THE LID TO THE CHEST WAS HELD CLOSED BY A CIRCULAR LOOP OF GLASS. AFTER CAREFUL EXAMINATION HE DECIDED THAT THE ONLY WAY TO OPEN THE CHEST WOULD BE TO BREAK THE GLASS LOOP. HE STRUCK THE GLASS WITH A SHARP BLOW FROM A KITCHEN KNIFE, BUT THE LOOP JUST BOUNCED A BIT AND GAVE OUT A HIGH MUSICAL NOTE. AFTER SEVERAL MORE BLOWS WITH THE SAME RESULT, HE FETCHED A HAMMER AND STRUCK THE LOOP WITH AN OVERHAND SWING. THE LID POPPED OPEN AND A GENIE APPEARED (YOU KNEW THAT THERE WAS GOING TO BE A GENIE. RIGHT? IT

SAYS SO, RIGHT UP THERE IN THE TITLE.)

IN THE MANNER OF GENIES EVERYWHERE, THIS ONE BOWED AND INFORMED GENE THAT HE WAS MOST HAPPY TO BE FREE OF THE CHEST IN WHICH GENE'S FATHER HAD IMPRISONED HIM, AND THAT GENE WOULD HAVE THE USUAL THREE WISHES. A BIT TAKEN ABACK BY THIS, (HAVING ALWAYS CONSIDERED GENIES TO BE COMPLETELY FICTIOUS), HE LOOKED UP AT THE GENIE AND CONSIDERED HIS OPTIONS. "ARE THERE ANY LIMITS TO THE WISHES?" HE ASKED.

THE GENIE LOOKED THOUGHTFUL FOR A MOMENT THEN SHRUGGED. "WELL, I CAN'T VIOLATE NATURAL LAWS, SO WHATEVER I DO WILL FALL INTO THE REALM OF THE POSSIBLE. FOR EXAMPLE, I CAN SEE THAT YOU ARE THINKING THAT I CAN JUST MAKE THE VOTE FOR YOU TO BE OVERWHELMINGLY IN YOUR FAVOR. I COULD DO THAT, BUT A COMPARISON WITH EXIT POLLS WOULD REVEAL THAT THE BALLOTS WERE TAMPERED WITH."

"SO I NEED TO BE MORE — AH ROUNDABOUT."

"YOU COULD PUT IT THAT WAY," THE GENIE CONFIRMED.

"WELL," GENE DRUMMED HIS FINGERS ON THE TABLE FOR A MOMENT. "ONE OF THE PROBLEMS I'VE BEEN HAVING IS THAT THE PEOPLE JUST DON'T UNDERSTAND THAT I HAVE THEIR BEST INTERESTS AT HEART, THAT I KNOW WHAT PROGRAMS AND LAWS THAT THEY NEED. IN SHORT, THE ELECTORATE ISN'T TOO BRIGHT. COULD YOU MAKE ALL OF THE VOTERS IN THE STATE MORE INTELLIGENT?"

THE GENIE CONSIDERED THAT FOR A BIT.

"Well, that's some genetic manipulation on a pretty big scale, but I can do it."

"Great," Gene exclaimed, "do it!"

The genie grunted, furrowed his brow for a while then brightened up. "There. Done! Not as hard as I thought either."

Gene was getting warmed up now. "Fabulous! The other problem, of course, is that the voters are lazy. They don't get out and vote; they'd rather sit at home, take the day off, sit on their sofa, drink beer and watch the results on the tube. Can you make them more motivated?"

"Sure," the genie confirmed. That's an easy one."

"Do it!"

"Done!" the genie exclaimed. "Two wishes down, one to go!"

"Umm," Gene said thoughtfully. "One of the problems I've always had — I suppose that all candidates have — is that of name recognition. People don't know me and don't know my record. I'm just a name on a ballot. Can you make it so that all the voters know me, just as though they have read my record and shaken my hand?"

"False memories," the genie confirmed. "Do that standing on my head."

"Well, do it"

The genie inverted himself until he was standing on his head, winked at Gene and disappeared. Gene shook his head, wondering whether or not he had imagined the whole

THING, THEN SHRUGGED AND WENT UP TO BED, LEAVING THE LITTLE CHEST ON THE TABLE BEHIND HIM.

***

ON ELECTION EVE, GENE SAT ON HIS SOFA DRINKING A BEER AND WATCHING THE ELECTION RESULTS ON THE TV. THE COMMENTATOR WAS INTERVIEWING THE LAST FEW VOTERS AS THEY LEFT THE POLLS. "YOUR NAME, SIR?" HE SHOVED THE MIKE TOWARD A PORTLY GENTLEMAN.

"MIKE. MIKE LOPEZ."

"WOULD YOU TELL US HOW YOU VOTED SIR?"

"SURE AS HELL BE GLAD TO. UP UNTIL A COUPLE WEEKS AGO, I JUST DIDN'T GIVE A DAMN, THEN SOMEHOW I GOT TO THINKING ABOUT IT, AND I REALIZED WHAT A JERK THAT GENE GUY IS AND WHAT A LOUSY RECORD HE HAS, SO I VOTED FOR HIS OPPONENT. DON'T KNOW MUCH ABOUT HIM, BUT ANYONE'S GOTTA BE BETTER THAN GENE." MIKE LOOKED AROUND. "EVERYONE I TALK TO FEELS THE SAME WAY. EVERYONE'S BEEN THINKING THAT WE OUGHT TO HAVE A 'NONE OF THE ABOVE' CHOICE ON THE BALLOT, TOO. MAYBE GET UP A CITIZEN'S INITIATIVE TO INCLUDE THAT IN THE NEXT ELECTION. PUT DOWN THE BEERS, GET UP OFF OF THE SOFA AND DO STUFF."

THE COMMENTATOR NODDED. "STILL, GOING FROM A STATISTICAL TIE TO 98 PERCENT AGAINST GENE IS PRETTY AMAZING."

"NAH, PEOPLE JUST WISED UP. HUGE TURNOUT, TOO, ENH?"

THE COMMENTATOR NODDED. "SURE IS. PROBABLY A RECORD."

262

TAXATION

Government quickly falls into the habit of using the tax to discourage some types of things and to encourage others. This is generally termed 'social engineering'. The concept of social engineering rests upon an idea that is repugnant to most people – that some persons have the right to dictate to all of us what our morals should be. The most egregious historical example has been an outgrowth of Prohibition and the taxation of alcoholic beverages. Intrinsically, most alcoholic drinks are only marginally more expensive than soft drinks or fruit juices, but the special taxes placed upon them increases their price to the consumer, sometimes to several times their intrinsic value. The excuse for such 'special' taxes is the presumed evil of the taxed product. There is an ongoing campaign to do the same to tobacco products. This, hopefully, does not explain the increased tax burden borne by married couples over their bachelor brethren. The imposition of "sin taxes" is very lucrative because they appeal to a moralistic streak in a fair percentage of the populace.

Of course government is always on the lookout for new ways to improve the morality of the public at large and to improve tax receipts as well.

The power to tax is the power to destroy.

All taxes should be specific – that is to say that they should be for a specific purpose, not to enrich the treasury at large. Most taxes, income, sales, excise, etc. are non-specific, which is to say that they go to a common treasury, from whence they are allocated to various projects. This places too much power in the hands of politicians and too many chances for corruption. Taxes should also be optional: only the persons who wish to use the benefit obtained by the tax should be required to pay it. For example someone, interested in a retirement income and trusting the government more than a private organization, could opt for a social security tax. (This would, of course, make it hard for a Ponzi scheme such as today's Social Security to operate.) The basic problem with this approach is the sorting out of beneficiaries, as things such as protection of the commons or the military benefit all. We should consider those in more detail. In general, however the system of "pay for what you get" works well for private enterprise and should work well for the larger government enterprise, with the caveat that the government would have no power to compel attendance or usage. Any enterprise, which became mismanaged or the subject of corruption, would quickly lose public support and public funds. Allowing people to vote with their feet is a fair assurance of honesty, as is possible competition from a private source.

ARMS

Political power, as Chairman Mao has famously stated, grows out of the barrel of a gun. Regardless of what one thinks of dictators, mass murderers or the communist Chairmen's little red book, the observation is both accurate and true. The founding fathers of the United States understood this truism very well, long before Mao was born, having just fought and won an insurrection, and therefore protected the natural right to bear arms, putting it beyond the meddlesome power of government by placing it in the Bill of Rights. The intent of so protecting this right was well expressed by Jefferson: "The tree of Liberty must be refreshed from time to time with the blood of patriots and tyrants. It is its natural manure."

Now understand that the thought of an armed populace is something that makes politicians and their governments nervous, and the more wrongs they commit, the more power they corral to themselves, the more nervous they become. This nervousness translates itself into persistent attempts to dismantle, circumvent or limit the ability of the public at large to go armed. The presence and extent of these attempts is a fair measure of the level of nervousness and therefore an indirect measure of wrongdoings.

In the first century of this country nobody questioned the right to go armed. Gentlemen regularly carried a Derringer in their vest, and even fine ladies would carry a four-shot pepperbox in their garter. Merchant ships went armed with cannon, stagecoaches always carried a shotgun and ranchers carried a revolver on their belt along with a saddle gun on their horse. Violence involving firearms was relatively rare – certainly less than in many of our major cities today, for everyone understood Voltaire's maxim that an 'armed society is a polite society'. In those days government was a somewhat distant and useful adjunct of society. Nobody other than a few outlaws, pirates and predatory nations feared the government.

When the sins of politicians and government in general began to encroach on society, there grew an equal general distrust by the government of an armed populace. After all, the Second Amendment had been placed in the Constitution with the exact thought, according to Jefferson, that the populace could rise up in bloody revolt against an overbearing and abusive government. If a politician is desirous of being overbearing and abusive, this could make him or her nervous, hence the propensity to infringe the right that 'shall not be infringed'. Today, of course, weapons laws have gone far beyond the fringe – indeed, they have almost completely consumed the entire rug, fringe and all.

It has been observed that when a government fears the people, the people will have freedom, but when the people fear the government, the people will be enslaved.

Presumably, according to our founding documents, the government 'draws its rightful powers from the people' which is to say that the government operates as an agent of the people. If this is truly so, then there is no right that the government can exercise that does not already reside in the people. If the government cannot trust the people to be armed, then by what logic can the people trust the government to go armed? The government should not possess instruments of defense or offense denied to its citizens.

Mao was right – an unarmed populace has no source of political power.

The Second Amendment means exactly what it says. The Supreme Court (by a minimal margin) has held that the right to bear arms is an individual right. It now only remains to decide what 'shall not be infringed' means. The government and the courts will dodge this question until they think that they have a way to parse it. We can only hope that when it does appear before a court that the court is conversant with the English language.

TRIVIA

Trivia is quite popular, particularly with legislatures and politicians (which are pretty much the same thing). The reason for this is quite simple: politicians, by and large, are an uneducated lot. That is not to say that they have not had an education – most are attorneys, sociologists and administrative specialists – but that they are uneducated about and indeed fundamentally unaware of the driving forces in the world today. These forces are science, technology and business. The concern of legislative bodies with trivia is mind-boggling. Hours are spent debating the question of whether or not creationism should be taught in schools and considering the problems of the use of drugs in sports. Special exemptions from anti-monopoly laws are extended to various sports. Local governmental bodies consider endlessly whether or not a new sports stadium should be built, at taxpayer expense, to replace the as-yet-unpaid-for stadium built twenty-five years ago, while the local high school teaches math at a level surpassed by fourth graders in China.

Here's a suggestion: go to Rome and take a look at the Coliseum. That's an ancient Roman sports stadium built at the height of the Roman Empire. It is still there. There is no more Roman Empire.

If government is going to be meaningful, it should address problems that involve the survival and improvement of the nation at large. Here's a news flash – sports, the treatment of animals, odd religious views, the sexual behavior of various popular figures, bogus science and the preservation of sparrows, frogs or minnows should not be of overwhelming concern; the education of our children, business, scientific and technological advancement should be. Anything else is a fast track to third world status.

Stopping to smell the flowers is nice – but if you do it while running a race, you will lose.

Legislatures that spend time on declaring national sunflower day and similar pursuits are wasting their time and the taxpayer's money. There are matters of substantial import to deal with. These should be delt with, then a recess declared so that one and all could go fishing or just have a beer. The country would be better off and wealthier for it.

OIL

Oil is an American thing. "Colonel" Edwin Drake in Pennsylvania first drilled for oil in the United States in 1859. For some years people drilling for salt or water in the area had found their wells fouled with oil and simply abandoned them, there being no commercial use for the stuff. Drake, however, had taken the trouble to have oil analyzed by a chemist, who found that a good lamp illuminant could be distilled from the material. That illuminant was kerosene, and the discovery probably saved the whales, long before there were environmental movements, since whale oil had been the lamp fuel of choice for over a century, leading to a massive reduction in the whale population. With the advent of the internal combustion engine oil came into its own. Kerosene and gasoline were the first interesting distillates, but a host of other materials followed as chemists began to play with distilling, combining, cracking and modifying the various chemicals that were available in the black goop pumped from the ground. Seventy-five years after Drake's well the oil drilling and refining business was well established and growing. Today all manner of things come from the wonderful stuff, from plastics and dyes to medicines and lubricants. The chief thing that we use petrochemicals for, though, is fuels. Gasoline for our cars, diesel for trucks and trains, JP-4 for planes and heavy bunker oil for ships. We move on oil derivatives.

There are drawbacks to this.

When complex hydrocarbons are burned we get a witch's brew of other chemicals from carbon dioxide to complex sulfur compounds, all of which are spewed into our air. These compounds are dirty, make smog, cause lung diseases, dissolve marble statues, smell terrible and are bad for vegetation; the unintended consequence of our use of these fuels. The 'climate change' lobby uses and exaggerates these problems to further their agenda(s), thereby stealing the attention that should be given to removing these nuisances.

Nobody disputes the fact that oil is a limited resource. How limited is wide open to question, but there is undoubtedly a bottom to either that barrel or to the air to burn it. Fortunately there are alternatives appearing on the horizon as our science and technology advance. Electric storage, in the form of lithium-ion batteries and perhaps even more advanced high-temperature batteries, is becoming feasible and the first serious all-electric cars are starting to appear. Natural gas, which will work with the internal combustion engine, is appearing as a reasonable bridge technology, while nuclear power for the generation of electricity has become a safe and economical source pointing the way to an electric future. There has become available recently small, compact, self-regulating nuclear reactors, not much bigger than a commercial clothes washer, capable of supplying 20,000 average homes with electricity. Government, at the behest (read $$) of oil, "environmental" and coal interests has placed any number of stumbling blocks in the path of natural gas and nuclear power. The government paperwork and approvals are so complex and lengthy that the approval process for a nuclear plant is over ten years while the permits for opening of a new gas field can extend decades. The government has also refused to license a "generic" nuclear plant, which could be approved for any place without delay.

We have had a good beginning with oil - - - it has kick-started our technological civilization, but it is time to move on.

Once again government has laid its dead hand on technological advance. Despite governmental advocacy of "green" environmental policies, there is no cohesive policy to advance us from oil fuels to other possibilities, nor is there any intention to let market sources sort out the best of the alternatives. Oil and coal interests have too firm a monetary grasp on politicians and political parties to allow this natural progression to take place. Oil has too many other uses as plastics, medicines, paints and thousands of other applications to continue burning it as fuel.

The odd thing about all this is that the non-fuel uses of petroleum are all much higher profit applications than the use as fuels.

THE THREE DEADLY VIRTUES

There are three deadly virtues that should never be practiced by government. Their names are **Equality, Charity** and **Compassion.** The problem, of course, is that the populace looks upon these as being good, as indeed they are true virtues when practiced by the individual. Unfortunately, though, in the hands of government these human graces become occasions of evil.

Equality. When, as individuals we practice equality, we try to see common humanity in each other, and reach out to our fellows while ignoring differences in religion, race, wealth and the thousand other circumstances that differentiate and can separate us. Sadly, the heavy hand of government botches any attempts at the practice of this virtue, substituting rigid rules, quotas and the pressure of political correctness for the true warmth of human feeling and understanding. Government versions of equality rob us of individuality. Insisting that a school must have seven blacks, four Orientals, an Eskimo and at least one handicapped student in each grade is *not* equality; it is stupidity.

Charity. Charity is, at its finest, an individual virtue. It may be as simple as a coin in the

Salvation Army pot, as selfless as the lifelong dedication of a medical researcher or as munificent as a Bill Gates' African outreach, but in any case it arises from an internal individual decision. Government debases charity by doing that which appears charitable on the surface – it legislates money to an ostensibly charitable cause, ignoring the pain and deprivation occasioned when that money was forcibly taken from those who labored to earn it. Government versions of charity are simply crude imitations of Robin Hood with a 40% commission. Further, since individual decision-making has been removed from the equations, they become the subject of scams, resentment, misuse, abuse and outright theft.

Compassion. As humans, we tend to have compassion on our fellows; we help up the person who slips on the ice, we stop to help at accidents, we visit an injured friend in the hospital. All too frequently, though, government compassion becomes a program to provide free or low rent housing to those incapable of caring for it, welfare to tempt young girls into single motherhood, a set of laws that empties the mental asylums into the streets or tender care for an insignificant minnow that turns the most productive farmland in the country into a dustbowl of dead and dying trees for lack of irrigation water.

Things that are virtues in individuals are frequently sins in governments.

We have a tendency to see things that are admirable in ourselves as being admirable in governments without thinking things through. We should regard government more like a machine than a human institution. Nobody expects compassion, charity or equality from a car; they just expect it to work efficiently.

SINS

Religions refer to forbidden things as "sins", but the mundane world of government and law does not recognize the category: religions have a somewhat different view of morality than does a government which must govern all manner of religions and atheists as well. Government does not much worry about whether or not you pray or whether or not you keep holy your particular Sabbath. Contrary-wise they do worry about your red light running and waste discharge. The number of sins in any given religion is rather limited, and devotees generally know what they are. This is not so with governmental laws, for we have legislative bodies which spend their time propounding and creating almost endless numbers of laws, which are then extended and detailed by bureaucracies and then are further elaborated by courts acting on the basis of precedent. The results are voluminous beyond belief, and it is doubtful if a single person could know more than a fraction of one percent of them. This is wrong. Religions have the correct idea – a limited number of laws that can be remembered and understood by virtually anybody within a sensible period of study. It is reasonable to presume that an encompassing set of laws, covering almost any situation, could be set forth within a hundred or so pages.

Consider the advantages of such a legal system: the law would be understandable by all, thereby probably reducing crime; legal proceedings would reference directly the applicable bedrock law without regard to precedents (after all, no two crimes are exactly alike), legislatures would only need to meet one or two days a year to consider whether or not anyone had invented a new legal sin (can you think of a new sin, legal or otherwise, that has been invented in the last decade? Century?).

Any such idea as this is anathema to politicians and legislators since it reduces their jobs to a useful minimum. It also reduces their chief enjoyment by limiting their power to extend control.

Society could be well governed by a limited number of simple laws.

An arrangement such as suggested above is looked upon with horror by those in power because it returns power and responsibility to the people, where it belongs. It is an article of faith amongst those of the political bent that people are incapable of governing themselves, much less controlling their actions. The elite must do this for them. They are, of course, wrong – it is the politicians that can neither control their actions nor govern themselves.

DEFENSE

The most basic function of government is that of defense; indeed it is the one irreducible minimum demanded of any government. It is a touchstone for the identification of a diseased and defective government that it turns against its own citizens, as did Germany under Hitler, Cambodia under Pol Pot, China under Mao, Russia under Lenin and Stalin and as Darfur does today, rather than defending them.

The means by which a government attends to its defense can vary greatly. Switzerland keeps a minimal military, but relies on a large armed populace for defense. Some need virtually no defense, not having anything that would be considered worth a conqueror's effort. Many rely on large standing armies for their defense.

In the cases of those that rely on large armies for defense, the tax burden on the citizens is substantial, armies being high maintenance organizations. Inevitably this will lead, especially during extended periods of peace, for calls to disarm, worldwide conferences on arms reduction (the opposing sides being equally desirous of redirecting their taxes), and suggestions of unilateral arms reduction. The problem with such utopian pursuits is, history teaches us, that wars are provoked by weakness and prevented by strength. For a nation to weaken its armed forces or to disarm itself in an unfriendly world is to disavow the most basic function of its government, the defense of its citizens, and is a blatant advertisement that the government needs to be replaced.

Those who beat their swords into plowshares will plow for those who do not.

A small military, in today's world, does not equate to a lack of power. Even a small nation with a correspondingly small military can project great defensive power. Nuclear weapons are the ultimate defense, and no sane nation will attack a country that possesses them. On the other hand, no sane nation that possesses them will use them, for fear of the ultimate retaliation. This has resulted in an interesting facet of modern warfare, heretofore unknown in history: nuclear arms, coupled with a delivery system, are a purely defensive weapon. If you own them, you will not be attacked, but you cannot use them to attack. Governments, the military and all politicians should understand this fact, as it is a game-changer. Despite more than half a century since Hiroshima, most of them do not.

PUNISHMENT

There is one universal problem that is inherent in the concept of 'Law', whether that law be religious, mundane, national or tribal; there must be a method of enforcement. Invariably, this means some form of punishment for transgressors and, in turn, this means some method of inflicting pain, discomfort or deprivation on the violator. Human ingenuity has seldom been more widely or more imaginatively employed than in devising means of punishment. It seems that our basest enthusiasms are aroused to fever pitch when it comes to the punishment of those whom we hold to have sinned against either us or society. Most of the punishments are of varying levels of barbarity, from stoning to stocks, and all rely upon the simple fact that we are hard-wired to avoid pain, which, presumably, will engender an effort to avoid future wrongdoing. The idea misses, and has always missed, a number of points however. This is confirmed by the fact that recidivism for most crimes, other than those of passion, is high. This has been true throughout history.

Modern psychology has delved into the problem of recidivism in the face of punishment and come up empty-handed in regards to a cure, but has discovered a number of interesting facts.

Firstly, it is possible, through operant conditioning, to install a strong aversion to the proscribed behavior, but the use of such conditioning is considered to be an unacceptable invasion of an individual's mind, since it makes basic changes in the personality. (See an old book, 'A Clockwork Orange' for a popularization of this technique.) Secondly, the individual makes a conscious and/or unconscious evaluation of the gains to be made through the proscribed behavior vs. the punishment, and, if the balance falls in favor of the behavior, recidivism results. This decision is further enhanced by the fact that immediate rewards are more powerful than distant punishment.

In days not too long past, substantial physical punishments were in vogue, particularly in restricted circumstances such as those aboard ships, on plantations or in small towns, where imprisonment was not a practical option. These generally took the form of whipping, keelhauling, maiming, confining in stocks or branding. In more recent times, as society in general became wealthier and able to afford the cost of imprisonment, jail became popular. Jailing has, of course, a secondary beneficial effect, inasmuch as it removes the wrongdoer from society and the possibility of continuation of the wrongdoing.

Imprisonment does to the soul what earlier forms of punishment did to the body, scarring and crippling it, and the person generally leaves in worse condition than he entered. These scars are hidden from the sight of others and can therefore be ignored. The fact that they are there is nonetheless recognized by the euphemisms that we use for incarceration : "Department of Corrections", "Rehabilitation Facility", etc. as though jail was somehow a cure for bad behavior. It isn't.

Prison cannot cure bad behavior and has a poor record of preventing it.

People who leave prison and "go straight" are generally found to have rehabilitated themselves, and the imprisonment was only a motivator. It certainly is within the capability of modern science, medicine, education and psychology to come up with a system of punishment coupled with therapy and learning that would turn the wrongdoer from his or her antisocial ways and into a free and productive citizen.

Although possible, no such system would satisfy the atavistic public need for a sense of revenge, but we should be able to set this aside if we could devise a system to substantially eliminate criminal behavior. This should be an active, and even urgent, area of research for the social sciences. No punishment should do irremediable damage or remove that which cannot be replaced if the judgment is found to be in error. We can replace neither life nor time.

RESPONSIBILITY

Politicians and government take many actions that impact people's lives, and in many cases, result in the deaths of people who would not have otherwise died. We have touched on a few of these in discussing nuclear power, pollution and DDT. There are of course many others, some only affecting a few lives. The problem with all of these lies in the fact that neither government nor politicians even acknowledge, nor are they held responsible, for these deaths. This is possible because government, run by politicians, exempts itself from any responsibility for deleterious results of its actions, while claiming full responsibility and credit for any and all apparent beneficial results. This leads to unfortunate consequences.

When individuals can take virtually any action and not be held responsible for the results, it opens the gateway to irresponsible actions, and many legislators are well aware of the opportunities that are implied by that dispensation. It is generally not a good idea to allow those who operate under laws to make those same laws, for who is willing to condemn their own actions?

Government cannot do anything illegal, since it alone determines what is and is not illegal.

Government employees, politicians and those supporting them should be held responsible for their actions and the results thereof. Anything less is an insult to the concept of the rule of law.

~~~~~~~~~~~~~~~~~~~~~~

THE THREE ENVELOPES

THE NEW PRESIDENT SURVEYED THE OVAL OFFICE WITH GREAT SATISFACTION. HE HAD FOUGHT HARD POLITICAL BATTLES TO ATTAIN THE PRESIDENCY, AND WAS, HE THOUGHT, JUSTIFIABLY PROUD. HIS PREDECESSOR HAD BEEN TERRIBLE, RUNNING UP HUGE DEFICITS, IGNORING THE POOR AND DESTITUTE OF THE NATION AND, ABOVE ALL, STARTING A MAJOR WAR THAT HAD BEEN RESPONSIBLE FOR THE DEATHS OF THOUSANDS OF AMERICANS.

HE WALKED TO THE FAMOUS DESK, PULLED UP THE CHAIR AND SEATED HIMSELF, SURVEYING THE ROOM, WHICH HAD SEEN SO MUCH HISTORY. GLANCING DOWN, HE NOTICED THREE ENVELOPES, EACH BEARING A SHORT MESSAGE INSTEAD OF AN ADDRESS. THEY WERE NUMBERED FROM ONE TO THREE. CURIOUS, HE PICKED THEM UP. THE FIRST, UNDER THE LARGE #1 AT THE TOP, SAID "OPEN WHEN YOU HAVE YOUR FIRST CRISIS" AND WAS SIGNED BY HIS PREDECESSOR. THE ENVELOPE NUMBERED #2 SAID "OPEN WHEN YOU HAVE YOUR SECOND CRISIS", AND WAS ALSO SIGNED. LIKEWISE, #3, WAS LABELED "OPEN WHEN YOU HAVE YOUR THIRD CRISIS".

HE SMILED, AND SLIPPED THE THREE ENVELOPES INTO THE TOP DRAWER OF THE DESK. THERE WAS LITTLE, HE FIGURED, THAT THE FORMER PRESIDENT COULD TELL HIM THAT WAS OF ANY IMPORTANCE, CONSIDERING HOW POORLY HE HAD PERFORMED IN OFFICE.

***

AFTER SIX MONTHS IN OFFICE, TROUBLE

ARRIVED AT THE DOORSTEP OF THE PRESIDENT. FIVE OF HIS BEST ADVISORS HAD BEEN CAUGHT IN A SCANDAL, AND THE MEDIA WAS HAVING A FIELD DAY WITH THE STORY. SITTING AT HIS DESK, HE SUDDENLY BETHOUGHT HIMSELF OF THE THREE ENVELOPES. CURIOUS, HE REACHED INTO THE DRAWER AND EXTRACTED #1 AND OPENED IT. THE NOTE INSIDE WAS SHORT AND TO THE POINT: "BLAME ME." THE PRESIDENT THOUGHT ABOUT THIS A BIT AND REALIZED THAT, INDEED, HE COULD BLAME THE FORMER INCUMBENT. THAT EVENING HE ISSUED A STATEMENT THAT, SADLY, THE CORRUPTION OF THE FORMER PRESIDENT HAD REACHED INTO HIS ADMINISTRATION, BUT, HE PROMISED, HE WOULD ROOT IT OUT SO THAT IT WOULD NEVER AGAIN SULLY THE WHITE HOUSE.

* * *

AFTER TEN MONTHS IN OFFICE, ANOTHER CRISIS ERUPTED WHEN A CHARITABLE ORGANIZATION WITH WHICH HE HAD BEEN ASSOCIATED DURING HIS CAMPAIGN BECAME INVOLVED IN A SCANDAL. SITTING BEHIND HIS DESK, THE PRESIDENT PONDERED POSSIBLE RESPONSES AND WAYS IN WHICH HE MIGHT DISTANCE HIMSELF FROM THE PROBLEM. AT THIS POINT HE REMEMBERED THE ENVELOPES AND OPENED THE DRAWER, EXTRACTING #2. LIKE THE FIRST MESSAGE, THE SLIP OF PAPER INSIDE WAS BRIEF: "BLAME ME". AFTER A BIT OF THOUGHT, HE REALIZED THAT, INDEED, HE COULD BLAME HIS PREDECESSOR, AND HE ISSUED A STATEMENT BEMOANING THE FACT THAT OPERATIVES OF THE FORMER PRESIDENT HAD PENETRATED HIS CAMPAIGN PARTNER AND SABOTAGED THIS FINE, SELFLESS CHARITY.

***

WHEN THE THIRD CRISIS ERUPTED A MERE ONE
YEAR INTO HIS TERM, THE PRESIDENT WASTED NO
TIME IN GOING TO HIS DESK AND EXTRACTING THE
THIRD ENVELOPE. THE MESSAGE INSIDE WAS AS
BRIEF AS THE FIRST TWO; "PREPARE THREE
ENVELOPES".

***

DONATIONS

Politicians, campaigns and political parties run on donations and public advertising, whether those donations come from the tax check-off on income tax forms or as lumps from well heeled individuals and even bigger lumps from corporations; even quasi-governmental corporations like Fannie Mae and Freddie Mac make donations.

Now most individuals are self-interested, which is to say that they do not go strewing their money about at random, but place it where they expect some sort of gain. Corporations are even more self-centered, and almost never dole out money without some definite purpose behind the donation. If it was otherwise their stockholders would take umbrage, and stockholder umbrage is not to be trifled with if you are an officer or board member of a corporation.

The truth behind all political donations, whether those be donations of time, goods or money, is that the donors expect some gain from the transaction. In short, a donation to a politician or political party is a tacit bribe, and if the politician or party wins the race a payoff is expected. If the donations have all been small and the donors very numerous, little harm results, for the payoff is generally in the form of some widely desired legislation. When, however, large donations are made by large corporations or organizations such as unions, the payoffs are substantial and most probably are of benefit chiefly to the donor at the expense of the public at large. Ultimately this means that the politician is only beholden to a small set of special interests, and he will endeavor to keep them happy at the expense of all others. They, in turn, will bend all efforts to support him. Down this road lies dictatorship and oppressive government.

Donations from the donor become obligations to the donor.

The political system of this country runs on a shallowly hidden system of organized bribery. This is tacitly acknowledged at all levels and, indeed, is somewhat formalized by official rules on lobbyists, who are often the conduit through which the arrangements are made. This is all understood on a non-explicit basis by the public at large, which tends to generate a cynical attitude toward government, politics and politicians. The one thing that does not make an explicit connection in the minds of the public is the reality that for every dollar slipped to the politician or political party, thousands of tax dollars are awarded to the issuers of the largess.

It can be fairly argued that no one person, organization or corporation should be allowed more than a nominal donation of time, money or material, say to the value of a hundred dollars.

This would, of course, not stop a politician from reaching into his own pocket to fund his anti-social hobby.

OLD SINS

Feuds between families and tribes certainly date back into prehistory; indeed, much of the Old Testament is devoted to such. In America the feud between the Hatfields and McCoys is legendary to the point that it has become a synonym for enduring familial disagreements. This unfortunate human tendency to continue disputes across generations finds one of its most egregious displays in relations between the descendents of African slaves and almost everyone else in the country. Many such persons blame their present problems (whatever they may be) on an oppression in slavery that occurred over 150 years in the past. This sense of blame can often be parlayed into guilt and the extraction of various advantages from those who do not share such ancestry, thereby furnishing an excuse for evading all manner of obligations and responsibilities for self-improvement. The very last African person, to experience slavery, in the United States was one Charlie Smith, who died in Barstow, Florida in 1979, having been allegedly born in 1842 as Mitchell Watkins in Liberia, West Africa, and sold as a slave in Louisiana on July 4, 1854. He was freed by the Emancipation in 1863.

The manipulation of guilt over historical

wrongs is a profitable business, the profit from which reinforces what is essentially a racist feud. The fact that the feud is perversely sustained and furthered by pecuniary interests is immediately evident from the fact that absolutely zero resentment can be found between Europeans and those of European descent for the extensive North African enslavement of Europeans, nor can any trace of a feud be found between African-Americans and the Islamists of the Mediterranean regions who practiced wholesale enslavement of Africans well into the 1900's, long after slavery had been abandoned in the United States. Indeed, many African-Americans voluntarily adopt Islam, the religion of these enslavers and slave traders. We should not try to create divisiveness between people to profit anyone.

There should be a statute of limitations on any and all historical wrongs. Two generations – 50 years, should be about right.

It is possible to create differences between almost any two arbitrary groupings of people on the basis of one or another historical event or wrongdoing. After all, the history of the world is one of immigrations, conquests, wars, rapes, pillages, mergers, migrations, invasions, emigrations, trade and other assorted adventures and misadventures by every country, tribe, race, ethnicity, religion and nation that has ever existed. We would be much better off if we just looked forward, rather than backward, for the past is dead and unchangeable, while the future is mutable at will.

THE PRICE OF LIFE

All things have a price. This statement is often regarded by the thoughtless, chattering class as being cynical and untrue, it being contended that there are certain things that are beyond price. The first of such things, it is widely stated is human life. This is usually brought forth as an argument when the price of such things as medical care and safety are being considered; the well-worn phrase 'it's worth it if we save only one life' often being trotted out as a justification for another expenditure of public funds or the imposition of one more tax. The reality is that we hold human life fairly cheap.

The 55-mile per hour speed limit of the oil crisis resulted in substantial savings in life due to fewer accidents and fatalities, but those lives were not worth the inconvenience of keeping the lower speed limit. The road departments of many states keep tabs on various intersections and use a certain number of accidents as the criteria of when to install a traffic signal. At about a quarter-million dollars per for a traffic signal, this means that the DOT values a life in the $125,000 to $250,000 range. If the passenger seats in vehicles all faced the rear, rather than forward, it has been estimated that the fatality rate in accidents would be cut by nearly 40 % .

We do not mandate automatic fire extinguishers in homes at a thousand or so dollars per house, although this would save lives. These are all prices we consider too high to pay.

The fact that there are prices too high to pay for known ways to save lives means that there should be a determinable price that society is willing to pay for a life.

Like all things in this world, human life has a value. It is neither zero nor infinite.

If we would make a determination of the actual value that we, as a society, place on human life we would be in a much better position to determine the most effective allocation of resources and we would save many more lives. While this may sound heartless or cold, it is reality that we are dealing with, and when we throw billions of dollars into a miniscule reduction of risk from a possible terrorist boarding an aircraft, we ignore the thousands of lives that could be saved by that money if invested in traffic lights. In a very real sense, those who refuse to consider the value of life in realistic terms are condemning some to preventable deaths.

PROGESSIVISM

Progressivism is a socialist style of governmental philosophy that admires the principle of the ant colony, which is to say, ordered and unthinking obedience of all people to an organizing force directed from a sole source, that organizing force being presumed by its practitioners to be beneficial to the body politic as a whole. It ignores any sort of moral dictate or rule that in any way detracts from its vision of efficiency, a fact amply illustrated by its historical support of eugenics and deep-seated opposition to religious influence. It has, in the United States, largely co-opted and corrupted the classical liberalism, which originally was concerned with natural rights along with civil liberties and considered that government was meant to protect such.

Conceived in the late 1800's as an outgrowth of early European socialism, birthed in the early part of the 1900's under President Theodore Roosevelt, fathered by communism and fascism, progressivism was furthered by Presidents Woodrow Wilson, Franklin Delano Roosevelt and Lyndon Baines Johnson. As a philosophy, it has infiltrated and informed both political parties to the detriment of the Constitution and the rights of the citizens of the United States. It is antithical to the basic principles of free enterprise, entrepreneurship, and free trade while being supportive of regulated markets, government controlled business, government banking and proliferation of legal restrictions on all aspects of public life.

The philosophy finds great resonance amongst Europeans most of whom seem to favor socialistic types of government. While the cultures of Europe have great historical depth and tradition, we are not Europe. The American experience is different in both principle and history. We have been leaders in the establishment of liberty and the application of the principles of capitalistic enterprise. That has made us world leaders, world-class producers, wealthy and has given us a government whose duration and stability are the envy of Europe.

Progressive principles are favored amongst both parts of Europe: the part we had to rescue and the part we had to beat. Twice.

Progressivism is antithical to what America is. Its ancestry claims Marx, Engels, Mussolini, Stalin and Hitler. We should have no truck with it whatsoever. It has corrupted our political parties and our laws. The dismal historical examples set by European countries should be adequate forewarning for us of the dangers inherent in socialism, fascism, communism and their modern incorporation; progressivism.

THE THIRD WORLD

In the last 75 years the term 'third world' has come into vogue, denoting the assorted nations that have lagged behind the more developed powers. The term is very mushy and undefined, and necessesarily so, for the level of advancement of various peoples exists on a continuum ranging from extremely sophisticated to abysmally primitive. There are portions of the world that live at a level little changed from 10,000 years in the past.

It has become fashionable to contend that somehow the more advanced societies are responsible for the benighted state of the primitive ones. This even extends to the contention, in certain rarified academic circles that are only distantly in touch with reality, that somehow the advanced societies have produced the impoverishment of the poorer through "exploitation". This, of course, is risible. If you are going to steal, you should go where the money is, not to the poor. If a primitive society is sitting on a valuable asset such as mineral wealth, development of that wealth by more advanced societies generally results in improvement of the lot of the primitive. This is a simple historical fact, measurable in terms of the health, population and longevity of the uplifted peoples.

There is an ongoing perception, amongst the same elites and academics, that primitive peoples are somehow vastly more stupid and childlike than the inhabitants of the "first world", and therefore are unable to advance through their own efforts. It is therefore, the argument goes, that those in more advanced societies are obligated to help those in less developed areas, usually by transfers of money. Of course considerable amounts of that money scrape off on the advocates of this viewpoint.

The inhabitants of the 'third world' are humans, as competent as any other people. They should not be tools of the charity industry.

Producing welfare dependents on either a local or on an international scale is a perversity engaged in by those who must find someone to be superior to. Those who find themselves in poor circumstances are a natural target for such and their receipt of charity assures the continuation of the predatory relationship. True charity would be to offer poorer societies a market for their products, not monies that encourage socialist governments and the maintenance of poverty.

PRECEDENT

The legal system runs on something called precedent. The concept of precedent is simple: today's decision is based on similarities to earlier cases. This is why the study of law is basically the study of what has gone before, and the memorization of decisions made in the past. Now this is an admirable system if one wishes to be systematic and organized but it has one serious flaw. This flaw is the problem of cumulative error. Cumulative error is easy to illustrate: suppose that you have a stack of a hundred metal plates in each of which you want to drill a hole in the exact center. You measure the location for the first hole very carefully then drill the hole. Rather than measuring for the next hole, however, you use the first plate as a template, placing it over the second plate to guide the drill. Then you set the first plate aside in your "finished" stack and use the second plate as a template for the third plate, then set the second plate in the "finished" stack, and proceed thus through the entire hundred plates. Now nothing is ever 100% accurate, so an error of 1/100 of an inch in the first plate gets transferred to the second plate and an error of 1/100 of an inch is added to the third plate, etc. etc. It is then conceivable that the hundredth plate could have an error as great as one inch, the sum of all the small errors. The same thing occurs in law when precedents are relied upon. The use of precedent in making legal decisions is English, dating to approximately the 1730's. Prior to this 'natural' law predominated. Natural law was based on the concept that laws should be rooted in morality and in natural rights of persons, and that any transgressions should be referenced back to such principles. In the mid-1700's, 'positivism' came to the fore, based on the concept that transgressions should be referenced back to the laws established by rulers. Machiavelli and others of his ilk were proponents of this type of coercive law. The use of precedent hearkens back to these origins and is predominant in legal proceedings and thought today.

One of the most infamous and egregious of cumulative error problems occurred in the Supreme Court in May 1939, (307 US 174), when the Court found a man named Miller guilty of owning a sawed off shotgun and moving it from one state to another, and supported the illegality of such an instrument in the absence of a $200 permit. The court thus validated the National Firearms Act of 1934, which seriously infringed the second amendment. It is notable that the plaintiff, the US government, was unopposed in the courtroom of the Supreme Court, both defendant and his attorney being absent and unable therefore to present a counter argument or take exception to several blatant falsehoods presented by the government's attorney. The judgment was made in absentia. From this distorted root has grown nearly 38,000 firearm laws in the United States, the error increasing with each decision.

There is little more in the general practice of precedent than judicial sloth and cowardice in considering basic moral principles.

Undoing the compound mistakes of a cumulative system is an almost impossible task – consider what would be needed to undo all of the law and all of the judgments that have descended from the poisoned tree of Miller. Basing each legal decision on solid principles makes law more difficult but it makes it more honest. Unfortunately it would make lawyers resort to reason, morality and logic, for which they are generally ill suited.

~~~~~~~~~~~~~~~~~

THE MONK'S TALE

IN A COUNTRY, DISTANT IN BOTH TIME AND SPACE, THERE WAS A MONASTERY OF HOLY MONKS. IN THE AGES OF INTELLECTUAL DARKNESS THEY KEPT ALIGHT THE ARTS OF WRITING AND PRESERVED ANCIENT RECORDS BY LABORIOUSLY COPYING THEM BY HAND ON VELLUM, USING QUILL PENS.

EACH MONK IN THE SCRIPTORIUM WAS GIVEN A TEXT TO COPY, AND HE WOULD SPEND LONG HOURS REPRODUCING THE DOCUMENT. ONE DAY A NEW MONK WAS INTRODUCED TO THE SCRIPTORIUM, GIVEN A DESK, WRITING INSTRUMENTS AND A SHEET TO COPY FROM. HE EXAMINED THE DOCUMENT HE WAS TO COPY, AND FOUND THAT IT WAS A LISTING OF THE RULES OF THE MONASTIC ORDER. HE ALSO NOTICED THAT THE PAGE WAS FAIRLY NEW. "OH REVEREND FATHER, HOW IS IT THAT THIS DOCUMENT IS SO NEW, WHEN OUR ORDER IS CENTURIES OLD?" HE ENQUIRED.

"AH," REPLIED THE REVEREND FATHER; "THAT COPY WAS MADE ONLY FIFTY YEARS AGO. THE ORIGINAL IS IN THE VAULTS AND IS MUCH TOO PRECIOUS TO BRING UP HERE WHERE SOME MISCHANCE MIGHT BEFALL IT. THIS IS A COPY OF A COPY OF A COPY, MANY TIMES REMOVED FROM THE ORIGINAL."

"BUT THEN," THE NEW MONK ASKED, "HOW DO WE KNOW THAT NO ERRORS HAVE CREPT INTO IT THROUGH ALL THESE COPIES, ONE AFTER THE OTHER?"

THE FATHER CONSIDERED THIS FOR A BIT,

THINKING OF THE ALL TOO FALLIBLE NATURE OF MAN. HE NODDED, "THAT IS A GOOD POINT. TONIGHT I WILL GO DOWN TO THE VAULT WITH THIS COPY OF THE RULES OF OUR ORDER AND COMPARE THEM WITH THE ORIGINAL."

THE NEXT MORNING, THE REVEREND FATHER WAS NOT AT BREAKFAST, AND ALL THE MONKS BEGAN TO WORRY ABOUT HIM, SINCE HE WAS RATHER OLD, FEARING THAT SOME ACCIDENT MAY HAVE BEFALLEN HIM. THEY THEREFORE ORGANIZED A SEARCH, WHICH EVENTUALLY DISCOVERED HIM IN THE VAULTS, WHERE HE WAS MOANING AND BANGING HIS HEAD ON THE WALL, CRYING ALL THE WHILE.

"OH NO, NO, NO. SOMEONE DROPPED AN 'R'. THE WORD WAS CELEBRATE!"

~~~~~~~~~~~~~~~~~~~~~~~

FREE TRADE

Free trade is pretty much a self-explanatory term. Trade between persons, corporations and nations, is the basis of prosperity for all. When you go to the market and shop for the best buy, balancing price, quality and a host of other factors against your means to make a selection, you are engaging in free trade. Companies, states and nations do the same thing, simply on a different scale. The problem arises when governments become involved, for governments, through their politicians, are subject to pressures from their constituencies and from their own perceived needs. They therefore use their power to interfere with the "free" part of free trade, imposing tariffs, import duties, taxes, etc. etc. on one or the other party involved in the trade. The fact that their own citizens plead many of these impositions does not change their nature. They are still potholes in the roadway of trade.

The basic problem, of course, is that governments, almost without exception, neither believe in, nor do they understand, the "free" part of free trade. Politicians (and governments) attempt to conceal this distrust of free people trading freely for their own benefit under such phrases as 'a level playing field' or 'protecting workers'. (An aside: have you ever noticed that the term 'workers' is associated with socialist or communist societies, while free market societies usually refer to 'employees'?) Free trade between parties engenders a strong bond that tends to preserve the peace, since those parties generally want to continue the relationship from which both are profiting. Interference with such relationships tends to produce tensions, discord and sometimes war. Private parties seldom interfere gratuitously with such relationships, but government frequently does, sensing money and power in such interference.

Although the Constitution gave the power to the government to make international trade arrangements, it is not always a good idea to employ the power. Often the best results will come from a studied neglect, allowing individuals and companies to arrange their own trade arrangements.

Basically, the argument against free trade is a disbelief in freedom.

The political propensity to try and tax everything is increased exponentially when it is something that moves, and trade involves movement, even if the movement is only of money. States try to tax sales made over the Internet, the country tries to lay tariffs on imports and exports and makes 'favored nations' deals with various countries.

All of these acts tend to slow down trade, impoverish the people and destroy businesses. They can bring on recessions and turn recessions into depressions. They should be eliminated. People are smart enough to watch out for their own welfare, politicians are not.

DEMOCRATIC CAPITALISM

Allow me to begin this exposition with a caveat: the word, 'capitalism', is a term introduced by Marx to describe the use of productive property to produce profit. The American term 'capitalism', as it is used here, refers to a system of free trade coupled with the right to own, buy, produce and sell property or products by either individuals or groups of individuals. By this definition, of course, the U.S. is not a purely capitalistic economy; it is a mixed one. There has probably never been a pure capitalistic economy.

The United States has long prided itself on being a capitalistic powerhouse. The attribution of the source for this has been to point to the fact that we have a certain amount of freedom and democracy and, it is postulated, capitalism can only exist in a free democratic country, since the essence of capitalism is the freedom to trade, set prices and deal to mutual advantage.

Unfortunately, this postulate does not stand up to the real-world test of observable reality.

Today other nations are beating us at the capitalistic trade game, and some of them are fierce competitors. China, a *communist governed* nation is quickly overtaking the

United States and beating it in the arena of free trade. All of the voluble protests that China (and India and Cambodia and Korea and Viet Nam, etc. etc) use "slave labor" (meaning relatively low wage labor) are beside the point. Labor is as much a commodity as a deposit of iron ore or an oil field, and a system of free trade will make use of it while lifting the standard of living of that "slave labor". These newcomers to the game are proving, once again, that free trade is the most effective system ever invented for generating wealth and raising living standards. There does not, however, appear to be any certain relationship between governmental systems and the successful practice of capitalism when dictatorships, democracies and communists alike can profit from it.

It is hopeful that countries that practice free trade might become more democratic, but that depends on whether or not democratic systems at large provide observable advantages others want. Currently, the jury is out on that.

Capitalism is simply another skill set. Anyone who understands it can use it.

As a country, we need to guard our free trade heritage, protecting it against not only those who would trade it in for National Socialism, communism or fascism, but also from those malpractitioners of capitalism that buy, trade and sell businesses and complex financial instruments without generating a dime's worth of product. We are probably one of the countries most skilled in the capitalistic system. We should not give up the advantage.

THE RULE OF LAW

Laws and the respect of those laws, along with a government that evenhandedly enforces those laws, underpin freedom. Laws that affect one person or group of persons but not another are unjust on a basic level, and are irredeemably wicked. Fluid and changeable laws ("living" is a favorite term amongst those seeking such) are destructive of civilization, trade and order. We would never stand for this sort of changeable rules in, say, football (oh – your uniforms are blue, so field goals will count for four points for your team) or baseball (no, your average team height is greater than the other team, so your pitcher has to stand on second base), yet we agree with equally idiotic civil law changes. The number of laws that are either inequitable on their face, mutable according to circumstance or are uneven in their application is absolutely amazing. It would not be an exaggeration to state that a majority of laws fall into either one or the other category.

The reason that laws are made unequal and the reason that the inequity is accepted is fairly simple – someone benefits from the inequity and those beneficiaries are more visible and have the ear or pocketbook of political power brokers, while those discommoded by the unequal laws are either powerless, hidden or both. In a legal climate such as this, one class of persons, say farmers, have special laws that reward them with monetary largess simply for being farmers, while another class of persons are made to yield the money, simply because they are *not* farmers.

The problem is exacerbated by the fact that the guiding set of laws, the Constitution, intended to control the actions of legislators, is also subjected to the same type of fluidity. This is the ultimate corruption.

There can be no rule of law unless the law is fixed and applies to everyone equally.

The creation of a law, or the corruption of an existing law to make it "elastic" or "living", or to keep it from applying to all persons equally should be given the shortest of shrift. Laws that divide people into classes or categories for the purpose of unequal treatment is divisive, prejudicial and flies in the face of the concept that 'all men are created equal'. The establishment of any given law that does not apply equally to all or that is not fixed should be held as a legal argument for automatically invalidating it. The majority of tax laws are of this type.

FORETELLINGS

The political arena is a popular place for foretelling the future. The candidate will tell us how disaster awaits if his or her programs aren't enacted and what ill effects will result from the opponent's suggested programs. In general the populace reacts to all of these with the blasé understanding that this is all so much political hot air. Sad to say, though, some of these predictions take on a life of their own and, like a snowball rolling downhill, grow in size and momentum. These provide attractive transportation for a variety of politicians. When the occasional foretelling proves to have some truth connected to it, those politicians who caught the ride will be lionized as foresighted and wise, but when the foretelling proves (as most do) to be so much bombast, the riders will discount their approval and recall their private doubts.

There is a touchstone to identify those foretellings that may have some validity and those that are most likely B.S. That touchstone is the level of knowledge in the field wherein the prediction is being made along with the technical acumen of the predictor. When an agricultural expert predicts a bumper crop of pecans for the year, we can have reasonable faith in his prediction. When Al Gore, an expert on nothing, predicts about global warming, a science besotted with scanty data and questionable theories, we must perforce discount his prescience. Metrological technology cannot even make reasonably accurate predictions of next month's weather. It is further notable that the agricultural expert has no secondary purpose – he simply wants to accurately forecast a crop yield. Al Gore has a political agenda.

One type of prediction is especially egregious: the political prediction. Political predictions generally take the form 'if we don't do thus and so, then these bad things will happen'. This type of prediction is proffered in an attempt to generate a fear of the predicted consequences and acquiescence to the suggested behavior. Very frequently thoughtful examination of the proposition will show that there is little or no relation between the suggested behavior and the proposed solution - - - that the entire 'prediction' is simply yet another attempt at political manipulation.

Predictions made in a field where predictions are impossible are a sure indicator of a con job and ulterior motives.

We need to intellectually divorce politics from junk science, and recognize a political and media-driven program for what it is: an attempt to stampede the citizens into accepting a position that they would distain if it were to be presented logically and calmly.

WAGES

For whatever reason, the sages that frequent the halls of government feel that they have the wisdom to determine, at long distance, and without regard to particulars, the value of some people's work. It is thus that they enact minimum wage laws. They never seem to stop to consider that a person's output value might be below the minimum wage, thus denying that person the ability to ever get a job. In all probability, these politicians *do* consider that, and are pleased that they have favored unions, who can now demand higher wages for their workers, have found approbation amongst those who cannot think far enough into complexity to appreciate the effects of such laws, and have added a few more persons to the rolls of government welfare dependency thereby locking in those votes to those who would increase government welfare programs.

Jobs, however humble, create wealth, pay wages, increase skills and learning and enhance dignity and self-worth. No reasonable employer will or should provide a job that pays more than the value the job creates – to do so is to create a lie. The minimum wage does not affect the person with even moderate skills, but almost any job will teach a person those skills. Minimum wage destroys these learning opportunities.

Minimum wage laws destroy the first rungs on the ladder of self-sufficiency.

The facts here are simple, and should be attended by every legislator and politician: minimum wage laws destroy the work ethic and create poverty. Those who foster them, approve of them and enact them are simply poverty pimps, pushing a societal and human evil.

THE THREE WITCHES

Shakespeare's Macbeth, flush with victory, met three witches who tempted him into murder and ultimate ruination.

In politics there are also three witches; their names are **socialism**, **progressivism** and **communism**; like Macbeth's witches, they tempt politicians. Unfortunately for us, the ruination that they produce spreads far beyond the personal. It is a bit of a mystery why the three witches of politics should prove so seductive to those engaged in the public arena, but the lure is unmistakable. Perhaps they are the political equivalent of a date rape drug, a fast and easy way to capture the vote from an undiscerning public. If that is the case then the voting public needs to be educated, much as we warn young girls about sexual predators. Regardless of the attraction, the fact remains that these three political philosophies have caused more misery and bloodshed than the worst of the plagues that have stalked mankind. Hitler, Stalin, Lenin, Mao, Pol Pot and many lesser dictators have all been married to one or another of the witches The superficial attraction, of course, is that each of the witches appears to offer free wealth to the populace and access to power for the politician. In addition, the politician can rest comfortably in the self-deceit that what he is doing is good for "the poor", and that his actions will raise them from their sorry state. The historical truth is that there is no surer or more direct route to general poverty for all, excepting the politician, who frequently profits handsomely from courting one or more of the witches.

The dowries of the three witches have always been poverty, war and death.

The old saying that those who do not know history are doomed to repeat it should be kept in mind. The history of the last couple of centuries, much of it still in living memory, speaks loudly to us of the danger in courting any of the three witches. We should be aware also of how attractive they are to politicians and avoid those besotted with their charms.

CO2

Carbon dioxide is a simple compound, one carbon atom married up with a couple of oxygen atoms. All things living or once living have both carbon and oxygen in their makeup. Most animals take in oxygen, use it to burn (oxidize) food and exhale carbon dioxide. Most plants reverse this process – they take in carbon dioxide, use some source of energy such as sunlight to strip off the carbon for building their cells and then exhale oxygen. For plants, carbon dioxide is basic foodstuff. This back and forth cycle is the basis of most life on this planet, and if we discover life on other planets, it will most likely be true there.

If you have a hothouse that is nicely enclosed, you can speed up the growth of plants therein and increase their vegetable, fruit and flower yield quite a bit by raising the carbon dioxide level in the air. A simple tank of carbon dioxide dribbling into the air with sufficient rapidity to keep the concentration at about 1400 ppm (parts per million) will do admirably. This level is almost ideal for plant growth. The current level of carbon dioxide in our atmosphere is about 350 ppm, which suggests that we are low on this gas. Unfortunately, the ocean is a great absorber of carbon dioxide, wherein it combines with water to produce carbonic acid. As more is absorbed the ocean becomes more acidic, and this inhibits the formation of shells by corals and shellfish. Many millions of years ago there was much more carbon dioxide in the atmosphere, according to archeologists, and plant growth was correspondingly greater. So how did the corals and shellfish cope back then? Pretty easy – there was a lot more available calcium in seawater back then, and the ease of obtaining it counterbalanced the greater ocean acidity. What has happened to all of that calcium and all of that atmospheric carbon? Well, all those little shelled creatures, the corals, shellfish and diatoms made their calcium carbonate shells, sequestering both carbon and calcium, where we find them today in huge fossil shell deposits, like the white cliffs of Dover, and no longer in circulation.

The carbon dioxide man pumps into the atmosphere will help plants, hurt corals and shellfish. What we ultimately decide to do is ours to choose, and is an example of what *real* environmental decisions are involved with. There are other options of course; for example, we could decide to calcine calcium carbonate deposits, release the carbon dioxide and return calcium to the ocean, but, at present, that is an overwhelmingly large project.

Environmental decisions are not one-dimensional; they are complex and involve tradeoffs. Beware of those who would simplify them.

Our self-interest would lead us to consider allowing a fairly high carbon dioxide level in the atmosphere. It would increase plant growth and might contribute a bit of a beneficial warming effect to the planet at the expense of oysters and corals. We should be vigilant about other effects as yet unknown. Sooner or later, and probably sooner, we will be into managing our whole planet, not just fish stocks and wild ducks. There will be tradeoffs, and we should make them logically and with care, not with one-dimensional and uninformed emotional debate.

ALIENS

There is a steady flow of border jumpers that come into the United States across the Mexican-American border. These people break a number of laws by the simple act of entering the country illegally. There are many politically correct terms that are used to describe these persons: 'undocumented worker' is a favorite, but in the final analysis the fact remains that they are illegal aliens. The problem is that these people are welcomed by a large number of organizations, amongst which the agricultural, meat, restaurant and food processing industries are predominant.

The government, while technically condemning the inflow, makes only feeble and sporadic efforts to limit the tide. The reason is not too difficult to understand, for this is a rich source of improper votes from pandering to an ethnic group. In addition, the aforementioned food industries contribute to politicians and political campaigns with an eye to obtaining a lax attitude toward laws and regulations.

There is a persistent canard that the illegal aliens 'do jobs that Americans just won't do'. The truth of the matter is that they accept wages and conditions that Americans just won't accept. This generally means hard work at a fraction of the going wage scale. The minimum wage is not enforced because there are few if any plaintiffs; the penalty for a complaint being a loss of work and deportation. The occasional raids that enforcement agents make, on the basis of outside complaints, generally report living conditions for illegal aliens minimally, if at all, removed from the worst of the third world.

The profits that come from less than minimum wage labor enrich a few companies, with appropriate amounts finding their way into political pockets. Time and again it has been found that, in the absence of immigrant labor, American employees were more than willing to do the work – at a fair wage. With the quiet complicity of the government, however, the practice of using cheap illegal alien labor persists in dozens of industries. The extent of the problem may be understood when it is estimated (nobody has accurate figures) that one out of every eighteen persons living in the U.S. is an illegal alien, a large majority of whom are Mexican. Countries that cannot or do not control their borders generally do not remain nations very long.

We once had slaves, but we have progressed in this, as we have in most things – now we have illegal aliens. They're much lower maintenance.

If we want to get rid of the illegal alien problem and border jumper problem, all that is needed is to eliminate the magnet that attracts them to the United States. That means getting rid of businesses that prefer to deal in slave labor by making it unprofitable. It is interesting that large numbers of highly placed public and popular figures deplore labor conditions in Cambodia and Thailand while ignoring the problem at home. It is probable that a fine attached to use of illegal alien labor, say, equal to ten years fair wages, half payable to the informant would bring rapid reform. The fact that such a simple law has not even been proposed demonstrates the fact that the real problem is corruption of the political system by private corporate interests, politicians and labor unions.

GOVERNMENT JOBS

Very frequently the government, or, more precisely, politicians of various stripes, come forth with a pronouncement that "xx number of jobs have been created". This statement is only superficially true in the vast majority of cases. The government may, indeed, have created (or more accurately financed) xx number of jobs, but that is only one side of the coin. The other side is that the money to create those jobs was taken from either the economy at large, inflation or from some special tax. The monies thus extracted will have two consequences: firstly, the loss of trade represented by the money will decrease overall prosperity and secondly, the decrease in overall prosperity will result in the loss of jobs.

There are two further dismal results of job creation from the rubble of job destruction. Firstly, the monies extracted from the economy are not all dedicated to the creation of jobs, for it is a necessesary adjunct to taxation that the expenses of collection and handling of the money as well as the misdirection of funds on the part of politicians will deduct from the amount actually available for job creation. This figure can be as much as 90%. Secondly, the wages paid for the created jobs are generally much higher than the prevailing wages paid for already existing jobs. After all, all government programs are either zero or negative sum games.

It should be noted that the average government worker earns, on average, three-fifths again as much as average private sector jobs.

Government job creation is nothing but an urban legend.

Politicians propounding government creation of jobs are lying.

What they are actually saying is that they want the public acclaim of appearing to benefit the citizens while actually damaging them. This fact should be shouted from the rooftops, but isn't, because all politicians of all stripes use the ruse, and the media not only accept the urban legend, but promote it.

EDUCATION

Education underpins freedom, prosperity and good government. The world today is far more complex than it was just a century ago and it is rapidly becoming more complex. Fortunately, much of the increasing complexity simplifies learning and the acquisition of knowledge. It has been said that the entire goal of education is to teach people *how to learn*, for once that has been accomplished a person becomes able to educate him or her self. Today the Internet, T.V., radio, fast communications and blogs offer us a readily available ocean of information from which we can drink at will and the person who has learned how to learn can quickly become an expert in almost any desired field.

A recognition of the potential of computer/internet-based education is overdue. Imagine the teaching power of branched recursive teaching combined with personal instruction by top experts, paced to the learning rate of the individual student. An investment in such programs covering all of the basic educational requirements from kindergarten to high school would pay huge social dividends and would probably prove profitable as well. Our present educational system is an outgrowth of the eighteenth century. We should remember the Biblical admonishment about placing new wine in old wineskins and revise our teaching to make full use of today's riches.

We currently have set the age of majority at eighteen years. It is evident to anyone, who gives it a moment's observation, that there are plenty of eighteen year olds who are totally incompetent to order their own lives while, at the same time, there are sixteen year olds who are fully competent to do so. The passage of time is a poor measurement of the ability to make one's way in the world as an independent adult. Would not a test to determine a minimal level of learning be a better determinant? Knowing how contracts work, how to balance a checkbook, make a budget, manage money and investments as well as being competent enough in some venue to earn a living should be a minimal requirement for being considered an adult. Having such a criteria for becoming an adult would lend meaning and a goal to education that would be likely to catch the attention of students, unlike the attitude of so many of those time-servers awaiting the liberation of a calendar date.

Education should be meaningful, result-oriented and addressed to the real world.

Sociologists have a term, 'rite of passage', that describes a socially meaningful event that marks the transition of children into the adult world. It is a significant datum that those societies having difficult, even painful rites of passage, have greater social cohesion than those with lesser rites. The United States has virtually no rites of passage. The nearest it comes to such is the issuance of a driver's license.

It might be worthwhile to consider the effect of a national rite of passage in the form of a test to check out the ability of the individual to function as a productive member of society, and tying the passing of such a test to multiple privileges such as the ability to make contract, marry, own real property, drive motor vehicles and live independently; in short, to becoming an adult.

CASUS BELLI

War is a bad thing. Almost everyone agrees on that, despite the fact that it is a major human activity widely engaged in and disproportionately expounded in histories. In modern times, however, we have corrupted war by making what is frequently termed "limited" war. The concept of limited war is that it is somehow kinder to restrict the objective to something other than victory - - stop at the 48th parallel, do not cross the Elbe, do not enter Egypt, do not bomb the Vietnamese supply lines, etc., etc. The examples are endless, and each example has assured that there will be another war or another atrocity.

War is distasteful to all, and should be treated like a dose of bitter medicine: swallowed quickly and completely, not sipped then set aside for a later time. This is particularly true when one considers that a limited war leaves alive a wounded and angry enemy. Observe the attitude of North Korea regarding South Korea after the Korean conflict or the US and Cuba after the Bay of Pigs. The problem is exacerbated when, after a conflict, "nation building", in which the victor's values and culture are impressed on the vanquished, is undertaken. A century of socialist misery in

India as a result of British rule and the current unhappy state of Palestine are a few notable examples amongst many. Partially consumed medicine does not cure; partial victory does not bring peace. A nation may go to war at the urgings of zealots and dictators, but the tolerance for conflict is limited by time, impact of casualties and loss of treasure. This is an added reason that war should be short and effective; extended wars turn public acceptance into revulsion and protest. It should be additionally noted that a short brutal war, leaving a defeated enemy with the enormous task of rebuilding without assistance serves as an object lesson for others who might be tempted to venture into war. Would we have any of today's problems in the Mideast if President Carter had responded to the hostage taking by a swift and ferocious attack, leaving behind a devastated Iran facing five decades of solo recovery?

We should trade freely, be steadfast friends and a terrible enemy.

Wars are prevented by strength, not moderation, not weakness, not negotiation, not bribes, not sweet reason. When we station armies in other lands, interfere in the affairs of others, pursue military objectives in other countries, take sides in local conflicts, apply political pressure and create alliances, we sow the seeds of war. We should pursue the arts of commerce and maintain a limited but powerful military with the sole objective of protecting our citizens and property.

HEALTHY, WEALTHY AND WISE

The US medical industry is technologically the most advanced in the world. We innovate almost 60% of all new medicines, originate over 45% of all new surgical advances and have the highest per capita medical facilities in the world. If you are being treated for a disease or being cared for after an accident by our medical establishment you are 22% more likely to be cured and 18% more likely to survive than in 98% of other countries. This being said, you will, on the average, pay about three times as much as in any other non-socialized country. Those bent on socializing the medical industry continually point to the cost of medical services and to the fact that we stand 24th in overall health of our population despite the quality of our actual care.

The cost of our medical care is largely mediated by the cost of health insurance, which is why reformers almost always target the health insurance industry. Unfortunately, the health insurance industry is not highly profitable, showing a return on investment of about 3.5% overall. The health insurance industry, however, *is* a large part of the problem. From approximately 1941 the industry has been in bed with both the Federal and state governments, and is subsidized and regulated by both. Like the Post Office, Social Security and any other namable government program, this means that it is inefficient, overpriced, inexpertly applied and riddled with fraud and graft. It is the fourth largest contributor to politicians and political campaigns. On the average, you can cut the cost of health care by about 40% by simply paying cash. It is unlikely that a closer relationship with government will cure any of this.

An additional factor in the cost of insurance is the love affair that attorneys have with the industry. It should be obvious that when people are sick and being treated with admittedly imperfect techniques, not all will have perfect outcomes. When we go about cutting people open with knives and lasers, messing around with their innards, sometimes removing or replacing them, then sewing them back up while hungry bacteria lurk in the background, there are bound to be occasional casualties. Medicine is an art as much as it is a science. This is the ultimate Happy Hunting Ground for lawyers. What emotional jury cannot help but be swayed by the tale of the child who died under the knife or the young woman grossly disfigured by an unexpected drug interaction? The emotionally driven payouts are huge, paid by the doctor's or the hospital's liability insurance, and the costs are added to medical care. Some estimates, in some states, run as high as 22% of overall costs.

The actions of the government extend heavily into drugs and medical equipment, regulating, permitting and approving or disallowing various drugs, equipment and procedures without taking responsibility for the decisions made. This increases costs, distorts the market and sometimes delays life-saving drugs while people die.

Another huge contributor to health insurance costs is that insurance policies are frequently paid by employers and the government allows these costs to be expensed, a considerable subsidy through tax credits. This means: a) the policy gets overused since the employee sees it as "free" and, b) the policy supplies often unneeded coverage. A person who shops for his or her own policy with his or her own money will invariably make a more economical and effective selection.

There are a number of reasons that the US ranks so low in world health, but there are three predominant causes. Firstly, as a nation, we take poor care of ourselves when it comes to exercise and food. Secondly, we do not educate our children in health care and give them (or ourselves) regular checkups. Thirdly, we have different standards for our health. We classify a newborn, born with a heartbeat, but who immediately dies as an infant death, while most countries classify such as a stillbirth. We treat an advanced heart patient while others send him home with an aspirin, to die a "natural" death. These differences substantially change our health ratings.

When government has its finger in an industry, costs go up, not down.

The cures for the expense of health care are several, and most are simple:

Firstly, the government should limit itself to simply keeping the health insurance industry honest, and shouldn't impose regulations on it or give employers tax breaks for supplying it any more than it does for the food industry. Widespread competition and personal choice will quickly drive down prices.

Secondly, as with all business, political contributions should be banned. They are simply bribes, and bribes have no proper place in either government or honest business.

Thirdly, any person being treated in any manner by any medical person or facility should buy his or her own liability insurance with defined payouts, much as one can buy flight insurance. The medical establishment and personnel should be immune to suit, the business being, like the military, inherently dangerous. Suing those who help rescue us from the jaws of death and disease is self-evident insanity.

Fourthly, responsibility for drug and equipment safety should fall on the manufacturer and be taken into account by the insurer (see three above). Even dangerous drugs can have a legitimate place in medicine. To allow people to die because a drug has a 2% chance of causing deafness is stupidity.

Developing drugs and equipment for the medical industry is expensive. Manufacturers must recoup their costs through sales. The government has a legitimate role in enforcing patents, and should not allow other countries to extort lower prices for drugs and equipment from American manufacturers by threatening to violate patents. This increases the prices to US customers and provides an unearned subsidy to other countries.

WHERE CAN WE GO FROM HERE?

As a nation and as a people we should place in front of ourselves a few goals with the intent to restrain governmental reach and power. Most of these are simply practical extensions of the ideas behind the Constitution. There will always be great resistance to the implementation of any of these goals, not only on the part of the members of the government who will be discommoded, but also by those citizens and businesses who have looked upon the government and its programs as a furnisher of free rides. When you hear protests against any of these changes, look carefully at the protestor(s), for you will most likely see someone who is benefiting at the expense of others.

Government should be a way for people to come together in order to achieve goals that would be prohibitively expensive or difficult for individuals to achieve, and which, for one reason or another, cannot be done by companies or other marketplace organizations. Placing other obligations, powers or functions upon government is the road to despotism. Rather we should strive to remove obligations, powers and functions *from* government. One of the chief concerns of Congress should be a search for ways to decrease and streamline government.

The Constitution is pretty clear when it speaks to personal freedoms. There is no reasonable argument that can be made against any of the intrinsic human freedoms mentioned in the Constitution, and the restrictions and elaborations that have accumulated around them should be stripped back to the basic rights enumerated. These rights are inherent in people and are not "given" to them by the government the way someone gives a cookie to a child; they are therefore properly immune to restriction or modification by the government. Any law or rule restricting any of these freedoms should be held void as a violation of the Constitution.

Taxes should be specific, that is, each tax should be enumerated and the income therefrom dedicated entirely to the purpose for which the tax is levied. All taxes, with the possible exception of the military, should be restricted and surrounded with safeguards, and *must* be elective. This allows citizens to vote with their pocketbooks, which is the most effective vote possible.

No politician should be admitted to any Federal office without being tested for basic competence and understanding of the Constitution, and should not be permitted to be in Federal governmental employ for more than a fixed number of years total. A fresh eye and mind is far preferable to political experience and is less corruptible.

Education is the bedrock upon which a free nation is built. Education should never be put at the service of propaganda, governmental or otherwise. It should be concerned with basics: literacy, science, technology, literature, mathematics, history, social and physical development. Obtaining of a certain minimal educational level should be required before one can be considered an adult and be admitted into the privileges of an adult, such as making contract, voting, owning property, raising children, marrying, having a driver's license, etc. That educational level could be reached at ten or thirty. There is no magic that suddenly confers competence at eighteen years of age.

There is nothing more that can be found in the elaboration of laws that have come to enmire various portions and articles of the Constitution than the fear of a free people by politicians or the petty concerns of those who would use governmental power to enhance their own private desires and goals. Probably 40% of all governmental establishments should be eliminated and a like percentage are probably unconstitutional under a strict interpretation of the Constitution.

The military should be for the defense of the citizens and their property, not for protecting our neighbors who are competent to protect themselves, nor for extending commercial ventures. The actual usage of the military should be brief, swift and devastating. The universal perception should be that it is fatal to be our enemy, profitable to be our friend.

Laws should be very limited in number, clearly understandable and taught to all citizens much as some religions teach a catechism. All legal proceedings should refer directly back to these laws, not to precedents. Federal legislatures should have as their chief function to occasionally winnow these laws and to consider whether the infinite inventiveness of the human race has managed to discover a new sin.

There are a few things that should be removed from the Constitution by amendment, as history has taught us that they will be abused by government. The interstate commerce clause and the takings clause are predominant.

Time and experience have demonstrated clearly that government of any stripe is unable to control itself when it comes to money. There should be a Constitutional amendment to limit the spending of the Federal government to no more than 15 percent of the GDP. Less would be commendable.

Our government was established to be a bottom-up institution. It has been hijacked, and is well on its way to being made a top-down institution. We should not allow this to happen.

~~~~~~~~~~~~~~~~~

"The issue today is the same as it has been throughout all history, whether man shall be allowed to govern himself or be ruled by a small elite."   Thomas Jefferson

~~~~~~~~~~~~~~~~~

www.ingramcontent.com/pod-product-compliance
Lightning Source LLC
Chambersburg PA
CBHW062123280526
45788CB00001B/36